MURDER
—— BY ——
GASLIGHT

MURDER — BY — GASLIGHT

LEONARD PIPER

GALLERY BOOKS
An Imprint of W. H. Smith Publishers Inc.
112 Madison Avenue
New York City 10016

First published in the United States in 1991 by Gallery Books, an imprint of
W.H. Smith Publishers, Inc., 112 Madison Avenue, New York,
New York 10016 by arrangement with Michael O'Mara Books, London

Gallery Books are available for bulk purchase for sales
promotions and premium use. For details write or telephone the
Manager of Special Sales, W.H. Smith Publishers, Inc.,
112 Madison Avenue, New York, New York 10016. (212) 532-6600

ISBN 0-8317-6154-7

Manufactured in the United States

To Mr Gareth Rees and the
staff of St Bartholomew's Hospital, London,
without whose skills this book would
never have been written.

CONTENTS

A MAN OF HIGH CHARACTER

A MAN OF HIGH CHARACTER

T hings are not always what they seem. We all know that. We all frequently forget it. Nature is full of examples of creatures pretending to be what they are not. Hover-flies pretend to be wasps. Stick-insects pretend to be twigs. The examples are almost endless. But still we insist on judging by appearances.

Every confidence trickster knows that, if you wish to cash a dud cheque, you should be well groomed and wear an expensive suit. We all know that. But still we are deceived by appearances. It is always dangerous to assume that because a man seems to be respectable and acts as if he is respectable, then he is respectable. For just such a man was James Canham Read.

In 1894 Read was thirty-nine years old. A family man. What else can you call a man with a wife and eight children? He and his family lived at 57 Jamaica Street, Stepney. Employed as a cashier at the Royal Albert Dock, he was responsible for paying out wages to dockers and stevedores. In all he paid out about £1200 a week in small amounts and in twenty-five years his accounts were accurate to the penny. For this he was paid £150 a year. He also acted as an agent for two insurance companies which brought in another £25 a year in commission.

To his employers and fellow workers he was the height of respectability. The typical cashier. Totally reliable. Totally honest. Rather dull. And yet, and yet. James Read had a weakness. That weakness was for women.

We are all familiar from countless films and plays of the complications that can arise in a man's life when he becomes involved with 'another woman'. The eternal triangle. So it was that Read's life became complicated. Except that, in his case, it was, geometrically speaking, not so much triangular as star-shaped.

Shortly after midnight on Monday, 25 June 1894, a Mrs Bertha Ayriss walked into Southend Police Station and reported that her young sister, who had gone out to meet a man at 9.15 p.m. that evening, had failed to return. This was a routine enough report and one which would not ordinarily cause the police too much concern. She was, after all, only three hours late and there could be a hundred explanations. The only thought that bothered them was that, less than a year before, a woman had been murdered in the nearby village of Rochford and the case still remained unsolved.

Details of the young woman's description were circulated but it was not until the following evening that any real importance was attached to the case. At about seven o'clock a young man entered the police station in a rather excited state and told them that he had found a body at Prittlewell.

His story was a straightforward one. He was Fred Rush of 17 Regent Terrace, Southend, the eighteen-year-old youngest son of a retired farmer. He had been to visit friends near Prittlewell where his father had previously farmed. Coming back, while walking along a footpath about three quarters of a mile from the village, he had come across a kid glove lying on the path. By the side of the path was a hedge, beyond which was a ditch and then a field of standing corn. He bent down to pick up the glove, which was in a good condition, and looked around in an attempt to find the owner. The path and the field on his side of the hedge were deserted but when he looked over the hedge, which was luckily not too high at that point, he saw the body of a woman. She lay on her back, head downwards in the ditch. There could be no doubt that she was dead.

Prittlewell was once a small quiet village. Then it gave birth to Southend in much the same way that a meadow pipit will occasionally hatch a cuckoo, wondering how on earth it could have happened. In the 1890s it had not yet been swallowed up by its hungry offspring. Situated by crossroads, with its church, a couple of pubs and a few cottages, it still offered to the eye a pleasant rural scene. A stroll down the hill from the village brought you to a bridge over Prittlewell Brook. On the right, just before the bridge, was the village pump, still standing to this day. On the left, following the line of the brook, a footpath led through cornfields for more than two miles to Brick House, Eastwood. The footpath was a favourite place for courting couples on warm summer evenings. Apart from them it was used by the occasional farm labourer going to or from work.

Prittlewell Brook is no small ditch. Its bed is six feet deep and seven or eight feet wide. In the summer months, especially those of a hot summer like that of 1894, it is almost completely devoid of water. Just a collection of large, stagnant puddles. The woman's body lay head down in one of these, the water stained red by her blood.

The body had been well hidden. It had been pushed under the hedge so that it had fallen into the deep ditch on the far side. Had it not been for the kid glove left lying on the path, months could have passed before it was found. The woman, who appeared to be in her early twenties, was well dressed, wearing a dark, double-breasted jacket which was unbuttoned. On her left hand she wore a kid glove which exactly matched the one found on the path above. Her right arm was doubled-up beneath her body, but the left lay across her breast, still holding her hat. Just below the left ear was a bullet wound. Death would have been instantaneous. The police searching the area around the path found a patch of trampled grass and a small red rose, believed to have fallen from her dress.

Once the police had finished their initial 'scene of crime' investigations, the young woman's body was removed to a large public-house, the Spread Eagle, near the main crossroads of the village. It was to there that Mrs Ayriss was taken to perform the unpleasant task of identifying the body as that of her sister, Florence Dennis. Having done so she returned with the police officers to Southend where she made a full statement.

Florence was twenty-three years old, single and had no occupation. Their father was James Dennis, a harness-maker of 145 Shakespeare Road, Herne Hill in south London. Having twelve children, seven of them still living, their parents had some difficulty in making ends meet. Therefore, while Mr Dennis continued working at Herne Hill, his wife kept a seaside boarding-house at Sheerness and they met only at weekends.

Mrs Ayriss was the wife of John Ayriss, manager of the Southend branch of Royal Express Dairies. During the autumn of 1890, while they were living at 187 St John's Hill, Wandsworth, Florence came to stay with them. One day during her visit, when the two sisters were walking together near Clapham Common, they met a man named James Read. Mrs Ayriss had known Read slightly for some time and introduced him to her sister, beliving him to be a single man.

After that, Read was frequently seen by Mrs Ayriss walking up and down outside the house. Although her sister never said anything to her about it, Mrs Ayriss thought that she and Read were probably meeting one another. Florence was then nineteen, Read had always seemed to be a pleasant, well-behaved man and the older sister saw no reason to interfere. Two years later, in 1892, after they had moved to Kingston-upon-Thames, Mrs Ayriss came upon a letter hidden in her sister's skirt while she was ironing it. The younger girl was out at the time. The letter, which had been written by Read, was addressed to 'Miss Latimer' at their old home in Wandsworth and was very affectionate.

In the spring of 1894 Florence had returned to Sheerness to stay with her mother. After she had been there for a few weeks she admitted to her mother that she was pregnant. This news came as a terrible shock to her parents. They both cared deeply for their children and were strongly religious. Further questioning revealed that the man involved was a James Read and that Florence had only just learned that he was a married man.

It was decided that, as there were young children in the house, it would be more discreet if she had the child away from Sheerness. Florence was therefore brought to her sister's home. This was now at 24 Wesley Road, Southend, a small, bay-windowed, end-of-terrace house in a short, quiet street lined with sycamore trees.

After her arrival at Southend Florence had written to Read, both her mother and her sister having seen and approved of her letter. Florence hoped that he might make some financial provision for her. He had always given her the impression that he held a senior position in the Royal Albert Dock. On the Saturday before the murder, in response to her letter, Florence had received a telegram from him:

'Meet 9.30 train at Great Eastern Station Saturday evening.'

She had gone out at 8.40 p.m. and returned an hour and a half later. She was bright and in good spirits. Apparently, while no financial agreement had yet been reached, she had reason to believe that one soon would be. She had threatened Read that if he did not do something for her she would write to his wife and employers. He had agreed to meet her again the next night at 9 o'clock.

Mrs Ayriss was out the next evening and did not return home until 9.15, rather later than intended. Florence had meanwhile been left in charge of the house and the two children. She waited for her sister to return and then went out. At about nine o'clock, on her way home, Mrs Ayriss had seen Read walking up and down outside the Great Eastern Station.

When her sister failed to return Mrs Ayriss became worried and went to the police. The next morning, Florence still being missing, she went again to the police and afterwards sent a telegram to Read. It was short and to the point:

'Where is Florrie?'

The reply was a letter, which caused her great concern:

Dear Mrs Ayriss,
What is the meaning of your extraordinary wire? Please wire fully. I have not seen this young person for 18 months, when you were at St John's Hill.

Yours faithfully,
J.C. Read

The publicity attracted by the case soon began to produce a number of local witnesses. Of these, the most important was a Prittlewell umbrella manufacturer, Robert Downthwaite. He told the police that, on the evening of the murder, he had heard an argument between a man and a woman. The man, whom he described as 'no youngster', had been trying to persuade the much younger woman to walk across the fields with him. She had not wanted to do so but eventually had complied. He last saw them as they went off together, arm-in-arm, towards the spot where the body was discovered. The woman answered the description of the murdered girl, that of the man agreed with the description already given of James Read.

Another witness was Richard Goulding, a gas-fitter's mate, who was returning home with his wife and daughter at about ten o'clock. As they were walking along Leigh Road in the direction of Solentine's Lane, a man appeared in the road in front of them. They had not noticed him before and he had not overtaken them. He could only have come out of the fields on the Prittlewell side of the road. The man walked quickly and at the next junction he turned right while they turned left. He had a distinctive walk and Mr Goulding believed that he could identify him if he saw him again.

Police-Sergeant Daniell reported that at 1.15 a.m. on Monday, the 25th, he had been on duty at Benfleet when he saw a man coming from the direction of Southend. The resulting conversation went:

'You are up and dressed early this morning.'

'Yes. Can you direct me to Benfleet?'

'You are in Benfleet. What do you want?'

'I want the road to London.'

'Where have you come from?'

15

'Southend.'

'Then you have come a mile or two out of your way.'
The police officer had then directed him to the correct road for Pitsea and London. The man had thanked him and set off briskly in the advised direction. The stranger matched Read's description.

As a result of these various reports a warrant was issued for the arrest of James Canham Read. But where was he? He was not at his home in Stepney. Enquiries were accordingly made through the dockyard police. It was found that Read had signed on at the dockyard at 10.15 on Friday morning. That late arrival had been expected. He had been asked, on the way to the office, to visit a fellow clerk who was off sick since his employers wished to know when the man was likely to return to work. This Read had done. He was last seen in his office at 3.30 that afternoon, but he had not signed off as he should have done. Upon checking his accounts it was discovered that £159-12s-0d was missing. Although a further £600 in cash under his control still remained, it was entirely in silver and copper and would have been a rather heavy and unwieldy load.

When last seen he had been wearing a dark-grey suit and a light-brown, hard-felt hat. His employers, when questioned, said that he was regarded as a man of exceptionally high character and studious habits.

The funeral of Florence Dennis took place at Southend in glorious summer weather. It was the kind of funeral characteristic of late Victorian England. The coffin was conveyed in a carriage pulled by black horses with black plumes, followed by two coaches draped in black, bearing the mourners. All the houses in the street had their blinds drawn. As the cortège wended its slow, stately way to St John's Church via York Road and the High Street, crowds of people lined the pavements, the men taking off their hats in respect. The precise time of the funeral had been kept secret in a vain attempt to keep away sightseers. It also took place at an earlier hour than usual to enable some of the poor girl's relatives to catch the steamer from Southend Pier. Florence was interred in the north-east corner of St John's churchyard which, even today, is still a quiet, tree-shaded spot in spite of the proximity of a multi-storey carpark.

But still Read had not been found. His wife received £20 in notes by post, without any accompanying explanation. Although, with her large family to support and very little income, she was already in serious financial difficulties she insisted on giving the £20 to the dockyard, believing it to be rightfully theirs. Her children had to be kept away from school because the other children were jeering at them, saying that their father was a murderer.

During the first week of July Detective-Inspector Charles Baker of Scotland Yard, who had taken charge of the case, received a report that Read had been seen on the platform of East Croydon Railway Station. It could surely now only be a matter of time. A couple of days later they found him. He was living at Rose Cottage, Fairgreen, Upper Mitcham with a young woman. They were calling themselves Mr and Mrs Edgar Benson.

At about noon on Saturday, 7 July, Detective-Inspector Baker went with Police-Sergeant Marden to Rose Cottage. They found a house that really lived up to its name, a delightful brick-and-timber cottage with a pretty garden and roses round the door. The policemen made their way up the flower-lined path to the front door and D.I. Baker knocked. It was answered by a pleasant young woman, but hardly had she begun to ask what it was that they wanted than a man appeared and gave them little chance to state their business.

'If you want Mr Young he has just gone across the green,' he said.

'James Canham Read?' asked D.I. Baker.

'No,' came the instant reply.

'I am a detective and I arrest you as James Canham Read for the murder of Florence Dennis on the night of Sunday, 24 June last.'

'You are on the wrong scent,' he was told.

The two police officers took their prisoner inside and searched both him and the house. They found a razor in a case, £48-10s-0d in gold, plus a quantity of silver. Also a copy of the *Daily Chronicle* which included a report on the Florence Dennis inquest and an envelope addressed to Edgar Benson, Rose Cottage, Mitcham. He was wearing a light tweed suit, dark-coloured spectacles and a straw hat. Upon searching the house they found a dark suit, with a revolver pocket, and a brown felt hat. They also discovered a further £35 wrapped in a towel under the bed. There was no trace of the revolver. As they led Read away, he called out to the young woman that there was nothing to worry about, it was all a mistake.

He was taken first to Mitcham Police Station and then to King Street, Westminster. During the journey he remarked to the accompanying police officers:

'Mrs Ayriss knows more of this matter than I do ... You can believe or not, as you like, but this about Southend is all wrong. I was considering whether I should not attend the inquest and offer to be examined.'

That same evening he was conveyed to Southend under the watchful eye of Sergeant Marden and immediately upon his arrival was formally charged with the murder of Florence Dennis.

The police meanwhile had been asking questions at Mitcham. They spoke first to Mrs Young. She was the wife of a curate and lived at Rose Cottage. Early in February, because her husband was kept by his duties in London, she advertised for a companionable lady or couple to share her home. Mr Benson had applied on behalf of himself and his wife, explaining that he was a commercial traveller for a firm of tea merchants. As such, he was away most of the week and needed a pleasant home for his wife and their child. Mrs Young asked for, and was shown, a marriage certificate. Everything seemed perfectly in order, the Bensons had moved in and the three of them (four with the small child) had lived happily together.

Now it was the turn of Mrs Benson to be questioned. She seemed to be totally bemused by everything that was happening around her. She could only believe that Benson had perhaps committed a minor crime that would soon be sorted out. She told the police that she was Elizabeth Kempton and admitted that she was not married. She was the daughter of a retired Cambridge printer and had first met Read at Gloucester Road railway station while she was employed in London as a confectioner's assistant. He told her that his name was Edgar Benson, that he was a single man living in Poplar and that he was a commercial traveller for a company of tea merchants, Peck Brothers of Eastcheap. He later told her that he had moved to 324 Mile End Road and this was the address to which she had always written to him. It was, in fact, the address of his brother.

After the meeting at Gloucester Road they had entered on a long correspondence and met frequently. During 1892 she had twice taken him to meet her father, but her father had taken an instant dislike to him. On one occasion when she met him at Dalston Junction he had been somewhat late. When eventually he arrived he had another man with him whom he introduced as Harry Edwards. It was later established that this man was his brother.

In October 1893, while she was staying with her parents in Cambridge, Elizabeth Kempton found that she was pregnant. She told Read and asked him to marry her. He said that he could not do so just yet, but would do so later. Not long afterwards he gave her a false marriage certificate. After the baby was born at Hallingbury they set up home together in Mitcham.

Being a commercial traveller he was normally away most of the week. He did, however, almost always spend Saturdays and Sundays with her at Mitcham before going off on business early on Monday mornings. Very occasionally he would be away at the weekend. These absences he always explained by saying that he had been to see his sister Bessy who lived in Canterbury. During June 1894 he mentioned his sister Flo who, he said, lived at Sheerness. He suggested that they might go and stay with her sometime. 'You can share with Flo,' he said.

On Saturday, 24 June, he had not come home to Mitcham, as expected, but had sent her a telegram reading:

'Cannot get home – have to go to Cambridge on business.'

All weekend he had been missing. Miss Kempton worried about him and no doubt about her own somewhat precarious position. He had eventually returned on Monday morning, looking pale and haggard. His moustache seemed somehow different. When she expressed wifely concern about his appearance he told her not to mind as he had been given a fortnight's holiday and would be spending the whole time with her. Most of the following fortnight he had indeed spent with her, only rarely leaving the house. The exception was that he was away on 29 June and the next day she received a worrying telegram:

'To Mrs Benson – Wire immediately if all serene. Not returning yet. Preserve letters unopened. Reply to Gomshall.'

He returned the following day but gave no explanation to account for either his absence or his peculiar behaviour.

When the police turned their attention to interviewing Mrs Read about her husband, they heard a story that was the mirror image of that given by Miss Kempton. They were told that throughout the whole of their married life he had always been the perfect husband and father. He had always shown her kindness and consideration and had never given her the slightest cause for concern.

He was, however, suffering from heart disease. He explained to her that, for his health, he had been advised to get away from the smoky atmosphere of London at weekends. He had therefore got into the habit of going to the coast for Saturdays and Sundays. Obviously, he would have much preferred to have taken his family with him on these little excursions but, given the size of his family, the cost made it quite impossible. He therefore went on his own but was always back home on Monday morning, obviously better for the dose of sea air. He would then tell her of the wonders of Dover or Margate, of the weather and of the people that he had met.

Searching the house the police found that Read's writing desk had been broken open and most of the papers taken away or destroyed. It was later established that, soon after the murder, Read had sent his brother a telegram asking him to 'take care of my papers'. His brother had done so. Not everything had gone though. Still in the desk were twenty blank marriage-certificate forms.

On 9 July James Read was brought before the magistrates at Southend for the first time and caused great excitement in the town. As is usual on such occasions a large and hostile crowd gathered to boo and hiss. Throughout the proceedings Read appeared largely unconcerned and made lengthy notes. The only time that he showed any kind of agitation was when he demanded the return of his money and jewellery. He was allowed the jewellery.

It is normally the case that, when a serious crime like murder is involved, any court 'fireworks' are reserved for the trial at the Old Bailey or at the relevant county assizes. With Read it was to be very different. The initial hearings were held at Southend and it was there that Mr Warburton, counsel for the defence, was able to make a name for himself before his more illustrious colleague, Mr Cook, QC, could get at the case.

It all began routinely enough with the prosecution presenting the evidence that the newspapers had already discovered for themselves or had learnt from the inquest: the circumstances of the finding of the body and the subsequent arrest of Read at Mitcham. The court hearings took place only once a week.

There was a little more excitement when, at the fourth sitting held on 31 July, Miss Elizabeth Dinah Kempton made her first appearance. She was wearing a grey woollen dress with a brown cape and a hat trimmed with brown feathers. She was slightly built, pale but attractive and with a quiet, lady-like air. But hardly was she in the witness-box before she broke down, crying bitterly. Some time was allowed for her to recover but eventually a female official of the court helped her to a private room behind the magistrates' bench.

A representative from Read's dockland employers replaced her in the box. He testified that Read was a quiet, peaceable and respectable man, generally liked by his fellow clerks.

The next witness was James Mahoney, a tailor of Commercial Road. He said that he had known Read for about ten years, principally in his capacity as a fire and plate-glass insurance agent. At about six o'clock on the evening of 23 June he had met Read in the Commercial Tavern. They had shaken hands and when, shortly afterwards, they parted, Read had said: 'You will excuse me, Mr Mahoney, but my wife is waiting for me.'

The Commercial Tavern is close to Stepney station of the London, Tilbury and Southend Railway.

Eventually, Miss Kempton returned to the witness-box where she told her sad story. Still hesitant and tearful, often barely audible, she had the sympathy of everyone in the court. Throughout her testimony Read stood watching her, smiling.

Next to give evidence were postal officials from Sheerness and London with copies of telegrams received at Sheerness during the middle of June.

June 11th Talbot. Chief Post Office Sheerness
Can you meet Saturday next nine reply fully.

June 18th Talbot Chief Post Office Sheerness
Meet nine next Saturday. Reply.

It was proved that the original telegrams were in Read's handwriting. It was also proved that the telegrams were collected from Sheerness Post Office by Florence's younger sister, Evelina, aged fourteen. During the period in question Florence had been at Sheerness. On the 19th, the day after receiving the second telegram, she told her mother that she was pregnant. She left almost immediately for her married sister's house at Southend.

Soon after arrival at Southend, Florence had written a letter to Read which was seen both by her mother and her sister:

Dear Sir,
I have left Sheerness and am staying at Southend. Please write what arrangements you have made. Address Miss Dennis at the Post Office Southend.

It was in response to this letter that she received a telegram arranging a meeting with Read on Saturday, 23 June.

The next witness was Mrs Ayriss, Florence's sister Bertha. Under prosecution prompting she told the story that had become familiar, the story that she told the police and at the inquest. How, while living at St John's Hill, Wandsworth, she had first met Read. How, during the autumn of 1890 while walking with her sister at Clapham, she had introduced him to her sister. She went on to tell of the letter found in her sister's dress and of the other indications that Read and Florence were meeting and communicating regularly. She then told of the events leading up to the night of the murder.

The next day was Sunday the 24th; my sister made a communication to me on that day. After that, I went out shortly after seven in the evening. I live in Wesley Road and I went down the York Road, up into the High Street, along Whitegate Road and past the Great Eastern Railway Station to Prittlewell and down the hill. I remember turning back. As I came back I heard a public clock strike nine. Then, near the Great Eastern Station, I saw the prisoner walking backwards and forwards inside the station approach.

It then remained for her to tell the court of her sister's departure to meet Read at 9.15 p.m. and of her failure to return. She told of her increasing concern and of her visits to the police station. The telegram to Read, 'Where is Florrie?' was sent at three o'clock the following afternoon. At the end of her evidence the court was once more adjourned for seven days.

The next hearing, on 10 August, saw Mrs Ayriss return to the witness-box to face Mr Warburton for the defence. For a while he contented himself with asking a number of perfectly innocuous questions. As a result everyone in court was taken completely by surprise when he bowled his first bouncer:

'You have been out to the Lyric Theatre with the prisoner, have you not?' he asked.

'Yes,' she replied.

The whole court gasped and sat up, suddenly alert. This, after all, was 1894 and for a married woman to go the the theatre with any other man than her husband could hardly be viewed as innocent. They could scarcely wait for the next question, wondering where it would lead. But it was harmless. Like a cat with a mouse Mr Warburton was enjoying himself, playing with his victim, certain that there was no escape. The next attack, when it came, was in a completely different direction.

'According to reports in the newspapers, you said at the time of the inquest that you thought he was a single man. Did you say that?'

'No.'

Another stir in the court as the coroner's deposition was searched for, found and read out to her.

'It is a mistake,' she said.

'Did not your sister know that he was married?'

'I had no occasion to tell her he was married.'

Quite soon he was once more probing the relationship between her and James Read. It was a business relationship, she said. He had been very helpful to her with business advice. Her husband was not very good at business. Considering that he was employed as a manager this was not a good wifely thing to say, her husband in court hanging on to her every word. He was soon to hear much worse.

'Have you had many letters and telegrams from the prisoner?'

'No.'

'Oh, come now.'

'No. Not any large numbers.'

'Well, how many have you received?'

'I cannot say. I have not taken account.'

'Not always in your own name?'

'Not in my name.'

'In the name of Dennis?'

'Yes.'

'Addressed as Miss Dennis?'

'Yes.'

Now followed a further series of harmless questions, easing the pressure momentarily, but only momentarily, because soon the full pressure was on again. Yes, she admitted, she had once been to his house in Stepney and saw him there with a woman and a number of children, but she did not ask if it was Mrs Read or if the children were his. With her defences now in tatters the skilled counsel began slowly, deliberately and systematically to tear her to pieces.

'Have you ever been to Buckingham?'

'Yes.'

'You met Read there?'

'Yes. I went there first and he followed a few days afterwards.'

'You lived at the house of Mr Bray, a grocer, and passed as Read's wife?'

'Yes.'

'I believe that some little time after that you stayed at Oakfield House, Leigh, as Read's wife?'

'Yes.'

'You previously made a statement that you had seen the prisoner, James Read, on Sunday, 24 June?'

'Yes.'

'That statement is untrue?'

'Yes.'

From now on, so far as Mr Warburton was concerned, it was a 'mopping-up' operation.

No, the evening of the murder she did not go out at all.

No, she hadn't really been surprised when Florence failed to return that evening because she hadn't expected her to. She had made arrangements for Florence to spend the night at a lodging-house run by a Mrs Edgar. She thought Read might stay the night with her. Her husband hadn't known anything about it. He was worried about Florence's absence and insisted that they went to the police. It was only during the next morning, when someone from Edgar's called and said that Florence had not been seen there, that she realized something might really be wrong. She had then sent the telegram 'Where is Florrie?' to Read.

Well, yes. She had known all along that Read was married. No, she had not thought to warn her sister.

It emerged that the affair between Bertha and James Read began with a chance encounter on Southend Pier in August 1889. It had come to an end when he met the unfortunate Elizabeth Kempton at Gloucester Road station. He now had a new and younger victim to replace 'the dairy maid', as he usually called Bertha when talking to his brother.

This devastating piece of cross-examination almost totally destroyed the evidence of Mrs Ayriss but did not alter the position of James Read. There was no shortage of other evidence against him and no shortage of more reliable witnesses than the perjuring Bertha. James Canham Read was committed for trial at the Essex Assizes to be held in Chelmsford in November.

A more immediate effect was that on the Ayriss family. John Ayriss had sat the whole time in court listening to the seemingly endless revelations and admissions of his wife's conduct with a mixture of horror and incredulity. Now, he acted. He threw her out of the house, closed it, sold off by auction all the furniture and moved away from Southend, taking the two children with him.

Innocent victims of the case also suffered. Miss Kempton's elderly father, hearing day after day of the disaster and shame that had wrecked his daughter's life, had a heart attack and died.

The effect on the Dennis family can only be imagined. To their credit they took in the now homeless and deserted Bertha but it can hardly have been a happy home.

The full trial took place at Chelmsford in November before Mr Baron Pollock, with the Solicitor-General, Mr Frank Lockwood, QC, prosecuting and Mr Cook, QC, together with the, by now, locally famous Mr Warburton, defending. After the revelations of the Southend hearings this trial could only be something of an anti-climax.

Read pleaded 'Not Guilty' to the charge of murdering Florence Dennis, but 'Guilty' to stealing £160 from his employers, the Royal Albert Dock.

All the previous witnesses once more paraded in and out of the witness-box and related their, by now, familiar stories. A few new witnesses appeared.

Mrs Schmidt, a nurse, was employed by Mrs Ayriss while she was having her second child. She testified that she had, on two occasions, posted letters for Florence. They had been addressed to Mr Read, Royal Albert Dock.

Throughout the trial the two defence counsel tried to shake the prosecution witnesses out of their evidence, entirely without success. If anything their attempts to bully poor Miss Kempton and to portray the obviously honest and straightforward Southend and Sheerness witnesses as liars only damaged their case.

Read still claimed not to have seen Florence for eighteen months. The defence tried, somewhat desperately, to build on this dubious claim by arguing that Florence's condition was the result of an affair with a soldier from Hounslow barracks. But, since they could not produce the soldier and also failed to produce any evidence whatever to show that she had so much as spoken to one, the tactic had little success.

They said that the telegrams despatched to Sheerness were not for Florence, but for Bertha. But, if that were so, why were they sent to Sheerness when he knew perfectly well Bertha was in Southend?

There was a little incidental excitement when Read's brother failed to make an appearance when called and was eventually arrested. But, generally speaking, the trial went smoothly and entirely the prosecution's way.

When Mr Cook, QC, rose to sum up for the defence he tried to cast doubt upon the reliability of the prosecution witnesses.

No evidence has been given to show that the prisoner slept at Southend, or elsewhere in the district, on the night of June 23rd. Instead of such evidence there was an attempt to give evidence of identification, but this could not be relied upon.

As to the witness Downthwaite, he never saw the prisoner's face, nor had spoken to him and knew nothing of the woman. It was true that afterwards he identified him at the police station, but such identifications are very doubtful.

Then, as to the witness, Goulding, he was with his wife and why was she not called? Besides, Goulding represented him as going out of his way, for he was going to Leigh. The real truth was that the Gouldings never saw the prisoner that night, but that Goulding, after the event, supposed that he had seen him.

As to the evidence of the policeman, Daniell, who had a conversation with the prisoner on the road, it was impossible that a man in such a position could have told a policeman that he had just come from the place where the murder was committed and was going to London.

Mr Cook also argued that there was no motive for the murder:

Even if everything alleged by the prosecution about his behaviour were true, while it was morally reprehensible he had committed no crime. If Florence Dennis had publicly denounced him, it could only entail him in an affiliation charge. It was not a motive for murder.

When it came to the turn of the Solicitor-General, he had a much easier task:

In reply to the defence statement that there was no motive, but to avoid an affiliation charge.

Would it have been nothing to have it shown that he was leading a wicked life, deserting his wife and family, depriving them of maintenance and wasting his substance upon women whom he has heartlessly betrayed? That he should be shown to have been, at the same time, passionately, sensually devoted to the third young woman, Miss Kempton? Would it have been nothing to have subjected her to exposure and to shame? The jury have seen her give her evidence with averted eyes and with broken heart. It was obvious that the exposure would, at once, have terminated their connection.

My learned friend has been able to give no evidence even to show where the prisoner had been on that Saturday and Sunday. The whole of that time was a sealed book, an impenetrable secret. And how did he try to account for it? By suggesting that the prisoner, having ruined that poor young woman, Miss Kempton, had made up his mind to desert her; was indulging in the intimacy of yet another woman, who in turn he would desert and abandon. That was the best defence that he could make.

When the jury retired, they took less than thirty minutes to return with their verdict of 'Guilty'. The judge then asked Read whether he had anything to say. He had a great deal to say:

My lord, I wish to repeat that I am perfectly innocent of this charge; that it is now two years since I have seen Florrie Dennis; that I have never written to her.

His statement continued in this vein for some considerable time but it did him little good. He was asking a lot to expect anyone to believe that he was the only one telling the truth – that the police were lying, that the handwriting experts were lying, that the postal officials were lying and that all the various individuals from Southend, Sheerness and London were all lying. Even if he had been renowned for his truthfulness it would have been difficult; for Read it was quite impossible.

The learned judge donned his black cap and pronounced sentence of death. Before the week was out James Canham Read was no more.

The story of the downfall of James Read is a classic case of a man spending years carefully building a network of lies and then getting caught in them himself. The prosecution was, of course, absolutely right about him. Had Florence Dennis really exposed him she would have destroyed the public picture that he had spent a lifetime creating. They would all have known. His wife, his elder children, his neighbours, Miss Kempton, his employers and colleagues in the dockyard. All would have learned that the James Read they knew and respected was just a hollow sham. He could not take that.

At the same time, his lies to Florence about his important position in the dockyard had led her to demand far more financial compensation than he could possibly afford. He was, after all, already having to keep two families going and that on a salary that was far from generous.

So what could he do? He was trapped. His position was desperate. And so, like desperate men often do, he resorted to desperate means. He killed Florence.

He cannot possibly have considered the consequences rationally because the chances of getting away with it were virtually nil. Perhaps he took the gun to Southend solely with the intention of frightening Florence; events then got out of hand, as events have a habit of doing.

At any rate, once he pulled the trigger he was already beginning the march to the scaffold. His chosen defence, that he had not seen Florence for eighteen months, could not possibly be expected to hold. There was too much evidence lying around waiting to be found. Letters and telegrams. People who had seen them together.

There was also Mrs Ayriss, a woman spurned. She seems to have been perfectly happy to sit by and watch her younger sister be ruined, but even she had her limits. She was also bitter. And so, with a combination of bitterness against him and the dangerous threat to her own position that he represented, she set out ruthlessly to destroy him.

His emotions early that following morning when, walking quickly through the Essex lanes, he turned a corner and found a policeman waiting for him with obvious interest, can only be imagined. His defence counsel attempted to make much of the fact that he had told P.C. Daniell that he had come from Southend, declaring that no guilty man would have said such a thing. But the geography of south Essex is such that, with the Thames estuary to the south and the River Crouch to the north, any man walking westwards could only have come from the Southend area.

Perhaps the most remarkable feature of the downfall of James Read was the sheer amount of destruction it caused to innocent people.

In the case of his own family, it meant that his wife was left to bring up eight children, many of them still very young, in a state of severe poverty.

The Ayriss family was irretrievably smashed.

The Dennis family was left in a condition of shock from the downfall and murder of Florence, together with the behaviour of Bertha.

The Kempton family had seen the death of the father and the ruin of his daughter.

All this occurred in a society which attached much importance to respectability and was unforgiving of lapses. No doubt, however, given the amazing resilience of men and women, the survivors of the Read earthquake eventually pieced their lives together again. We can only hope so.

THE LAMBETH
POISONER

THE LAMBETH POISONER

I n the summer of 1891 Lambeth, like much of London near the end of the Victorian era, was a fascinating mixture of grandeur and squalor. The contrasts within the small district were extreme. There was Waterloo Station with its great arched roof. From here could be taken express trains to the playgrounds of the South Coast, to furthest Cornwall or the whole spread of agricultural England south of the Thames. There was Lambeth Palace, its Tudor buildings redolent of its long association with English church history, Becket and More, Wolsey and Cranmer. Nearby, not far from the dark and murky waters of the Thames, St Thomas's Hospital, with a history almost as long, continued both to educate doctors and heal the sick.

Between these very different edifices ran roads crowded with traffic – cabs and horse-buses, carts and carriages of every description – and people, always people, the vast array characteristic of a great city. Along the roads were houses, some new and still relatively clean in the soot-laden air, others old, decrepit and smelling of decay. These were the homes of the people of Lambeth, as assorted a population as you could find anywhere in the city - railwaymen, costermongers, watermen, medical students, prostitutes.

These last, the unfortunate women, as the euphemism of the time called them, had not long before watched with a horrid fascination the cruel fate of some of their sisters, at the hands of Jack the Ripper, north of the river in Whitechapel. Although they did not know it, it was shortly to be their turn to suffer fear and agony at the hands of a cruel and merciless man, the Lambeth Poisoner.

It was on a wet evening during the first week of October 1891 that Eliza Masters met a man at Ludgate Circus, just down the hill from St Paul's Cathedral. She went with him into the King Lud public-house, warm and welcoming, especially for someone who had been standing for hours trying to shelter from the heavy rain and, at the same time, remain visible to any passing man.

After a drink together they went in a growler to her lodgings in Hercules Road, Lambeth. The man was tall, broad-shouldered and well dressed, clearly quite prosperous as her well-trained eye was quick to see. All right, he was not exactly handsome, with a thick ginger moustache and gold-rimmed spectacles which failed to hide his crossed eyes. But Eliza had seen worse and he did have money.

Later that evening they went together to Gatti's Music Hall in Westminster Bridge Road and there they met Eliza's friend, Elizabeth May. After the show the three of them climbed into a cab which took them to Ludgate Hill. But here the man left them, saying that he was staying at Anderton's Hotel in Fleet Street. The two women were less than pleased at simply being left to walk back to Lambeth in the pouring rain. Before they parted, however, the man did tell Eliza Masters that he would write to her arranging another meeting.

The promised letter duly arrived on the morning of 9 October. In it the man said that he would visit her at her lodgings that very afternoon, between three and five. He particularly asked her not to destroy the letter or its envelope, saying that he would collect them when they met. Eliza naturally showed the letter to Elizabeth May who shared the rooms with her.

That afternoon the two girls stood together at the window of Eliza's room, watching the street below for their expected visitor. After some time, as they peered narrowly out through the lace curtains, wanting to see without being seen, they observed another young woman, whom they knew only by sight, Matilda Clover, coming down the street. She was carrying a basket and had an apron over her arm. But what really interested them was that their expected visitor was walking a short distance behind her, apparently following her. As they watched the young woman glanced behind, giving the man a quick smile of encouragement.

The two girls were by no means pleased. This was no way to conduct business. Quickly slipping on their coats they dashed down the stairs, left the house and set off in pursuit, in the right frame of mind to tell the man precisely what they thought of such ungentle-manly behaviour. The little procession went down Hercules Road to the junction with Lambeth Road. When the pursuing girls reached the main road, noisy with traffic, they were just in time to see Matilda Clover let herself into a house on the other side of the street. The man immediately followed her in and the door closed behind them. The quarry had gone to earth.

The two angry girls entered a nearby public-house, had a drink and watched the house opposite, number 27. After about half an hour, with no more sign of life across the road, they decided that they were wasting their time and gave up the chase. Still talking angrily together they returned to their own rooms.

In common with many people in that rich city at the heart of a great empire, Matilda Clover lived on the edge of an abyss. She was twenty-seven, unmarried and had a two-year-old son. Not long before she had had a violent quarrel with the boy's father which ended when the man left, vowing never to return. He seemed to be as good as his word for she had not seen him since. Her position was desperate, life was intolerable and she reacted as many others do in similar circumstances – she turned to drink. Often enough she was taken back home totally and hopelessly drunk. Several times she had been seen by a local doctor, Dr Graham, who gave her medicines in an attempt to keep her off alcohol and dire warnings as to her fate if she did not.

Luckily her landlady was tolerant and sympathetic; many would have just thrown her into the street. And then there was Lucy Rose, the only servant in the house, who would often satisfy her own maternal instincts by looking after the little boy while Matilda walked the lonely, crowded streets.

It was while she was in these desperate straits that she met a man who was nice to her. A man who bought her new boots, a vital but rarely obtained commodity in that cold, wet city. A man who took her to the music hall where it was always warm and friendly, where she could laugh and sing and be, at any rate for a little while, a happy young woman. He said that his name was Fred and, all things considered, she forgave him his crossed eyes and that strange look that she saw sometimes in his face.

On 20 October, while she was cleaning the room occupied by Matilda, Lucy Rose came across a letter. Naturally, not having much excitement in her young life, she carefully spread it out and read it. She was pleased, if not surprised, to discover that it was written by a man. He requested Matilda to meet him outside the

Canterbury Music Hall in Westminster Bridge Road that same evening. It also instructed her to bring the letter and envelope with her. Lucy was interested to note that Matilda did, indeed, go out that evening, returning with a tall, broad-shouldered man, aged about forty and wearing a heavy moustache. He was smartly dressed with a silk hat. After a while they went out together again and Matilda did not return until between one and two o'clock the following morning, when Lucy was forced to get up and unbolt the front door to let her in.

At about three o'clock in the morning the whole house was woken by screams coming from Matilda's room. Lucy, accompanied by the landlady, Mrs Bowles, rushed to her aid. When they entered her room they found the poor girl writhing in agony. At times she suffered the most horrible convulsions, her whole body arching backwards. Dr Graham was immediately sent for but, as he was not available, his assistant, Mr Coppin, came to the house. Mr Coppin, who had no medical qualifications but was well aware of what Dr Graham had been treating Matilda for, concluded that the girl's agonies were caused by excessive alcohol. He reached this view in spite of the fact that, between convulsions, she declared that a man had poisoned her. Later that morning she became worse, Mr Coppin called again but, at 8.45, she died.

It was only now that Dr Graham, who had been out all night with a difficult confinement, finally appeared on the scene. With a report from the totally unqualified Mr Coppin, his knowledge of the girl's history, coupled with his own near exhaustion, he jumped to a conclusion. Without questioning anyone in the house he issued a death certificate stating that he had attended her last illness and declaring that death was from natural causes.

There was, accordingly, no post-mortem, no inquest, no police enquiry and, on 22 October, the poor young woman was consigned to a pauper's grave in Tooting cemetery.

It might reasonably be supposed that that would be the end of the matter. A closed case. A perfect murder. But now comes a new twist to the story. At the end of November of that year Dr W.H. Broadbent, one of the most respected physicians of his day, received a most extraordinary letter:

Dr W.H. Broadbent   London Nov. 28th 1891
Sir,

    Miss Clover, who, until a short time ago lived at 27 Lambeth Rd. died at the above address on October 20th (last month) through being poisoned by strychnine. After her death a search of her effects was made and evidence was found which showed that you not only gave her the medicine which caused her death, but that you had been hired for the purpose of poisoning her. This evidence is in the hands of one of our detectives who will give the evidence either to you or to the police authorities for the sum of £2500 sterling – two thousand five hundred sterling. You can have the evidence for £2500 and in that way save yourself from ruin. If the matter is disposed of to the police, it will of course be made public by being placed in the papers and ruin you for ever. Now, Sir, if you want the evidence for £2500 just put a personal in the *Daily Chronicle*, saying you will pay M. Malone £2500 for his services, and I will send you a party to settle the matter. If you do not want the evidence of course it will be turned over to the police at once and be published and your ruin will surely follow. Think well before you decide on this matter. It is just this, £2500 sterling on the one hand and ruin, shame and disgrace on the other. Answer by personal on the first page of the *Daily Chronicle* any time next week. I am not humbugging you, and I have evidence strong enough to ruin you for ever.

M. Malone.

Dr Broadbent, being a sensible man and never having even heard of a Miss Clover, immediately sent the letter to Scotland Yard. The police entered an advertisement in the *Daily Chronicle* as instructed and for a while kept a watch on Dr Broadbent's house. Nothing whatever happened, the good doctor received no further communication from the mysterious Mr Malone and the police came to the conclusion that the letter was written by some kind of crank. They therefore lost all interest and just tucked the letter away in their voluminous files.

It never seems to have occurred to them that it might be a good idea to identify Miss Clover and the circumstances of her death. Even the most rudimentary check could have alerted a curious mind to the interesting fact that the letter gives her death as taking place on 20 October, when it actually occurred early the next morning. This discrepancy came about because, while the poison pills were given to her on the 20th, she did not take them until she returned to her room, by which time it was the 21st. Clearly the writer of the letter knew a remarkable amount about the events leading up to her death.

Had the police chosen to investigate, had they spent just ten minutes talking to Lucy Rose, they might have saved a great deal of suffering. This poisoner was not content with only one victim – he had already found another.

At about 8.15 p.m. on the evening of Tuesday, 13 October, James Styles was standing outside the Wellington Arms, opposite Waterloo Station, when he saw a young woman suddenly fall face down in the middle of the road.

Dodging through the steady stream of traffic he went across to help. She was trembling all over and was obviously in considerable pain. She told him that a man had given her something to drink out of a bottle. The young woman asked to be taken home and, with the assistance of a fellow passerby, Mr Styles helped her back to 8 Duke Street, off Westminster Bridge Road.

While they were waiting for the arrival of the doctor the pain-racked girl, in between the most terrible convulsions, told her friend, Harriett Clemence, who lived in the same house, about the man who had poisoned her. She said that he had been a tall, dark man, with crossed eyes. The man had written to her, asking her to meet him at the York Hotel.

When the doctor arrived and saw her in the middle of an appalling, arched convulsion, he instantly diagnosed strychnine poisoning and advised immediate transfer to nearby St Thomas's Hospital. She was carried to a passing cab which was soon clattering off down the street but, by the time it reached the hospital, the girl's agonies had already come to an end. She was dead.

Police investigations found her to be Ellen Donworth, although she often called herself Ellen Linnell as she was living with a man of that name. A friend of hers, Frances Linfield, related that earlier that evening they had drunk together at the Lord Hill public-house. Upon leaving, they had parted outside, Ellen saying that she had had a letter from a man making an appointment. A little later she was seen talking to a man in Morpeth Court, off the Westminster Bridge Road, where the Shell building now stands. A post-mortem showed that she had died from strychnine and morphia poisoning.

The inquest into her death began on 15 October and was then adjourned until the 22nd. During the period of that adjournment the County Coroner for Surrey, Mr Wyatt, received a very odd letter:

To J.P. Wyatt Esq. Coroner   Oct. 19th 1891
I am writing to say that if you and your satellites fail to bring the murderer of Ellen Donworth, late of 8 Duke St. to justice I am

willing to give you such assistance as will bring the murderer to justice, provided your government is willing to pay me £300,000 for my services. No payment if not successful.

A. O'Brien detective.

The coroner was, of course, used to receiving strange letters. Some of them had, in the past, been very useful to him in getting at the truth. But anyone who imagined that the British government would be prepared to pay £300,000 to catch the murderer of a prostitute could only be considered insane. He accordingly placed the letter in his files and forgot it.

The writer, having apparently failed to excite the interest of the coroner, did not give up easily however; he tried again. This time the lucky recipient was Mr Frederick Smith, son of the well-known W.H. Smith. On 11 November Inspector Frank Thorpe, attached to Kings Cross Police Station, was on duty at Clerkenwell Police Court. During an interval in the proceedings, the presiding magistrate discreetly handed him an envelope. It contained two letters:

Sir,

On Tuesday night, October 13th (last month) a girl named Ellen Linnell, who lived at 8 Duke St. Westminster Bridge Rd. was poisoned with strychnine.

After her death, among her effects were found two letters incriminating you, which, if ever they became public property, will surely convict you of the crime.

I enclose you a copy of one of the letters which the girl received on the morning of Oct. 13th (the day on which she died). Just read it and then judge for yourself what hope you have of escaping if the law officers ever get hold of these letters. Think of the shame and the disgrace it will bring on your family if you are arrested and put in prison for this crime. My object in writing you is to ask you if you will retain me at once as your counsellor and legal adviser. If you employ me at once to act for you, as no lawyer can save you after the authorities get hold of those two letters.

If you wish to retain me, just write a few lines on paper saying 'Mr. Fred Smith wishes to see Mr. Bayne, the barrister, at once'. Paste this in one of your shop-windows at 186 Strand, next Tuesday morning and when I see it I will drop in and have a private interview with you. I can save you if you retain me in time, but not otherwise.

Yours Truly,

H. Bayne.

Madame Linnell 8 Duke St.

Madam,

I wrote and warned you that Fred Smith of the firm of W.H. Smith & Sons, 186 Strand, London was going to poison you, and I am writing you now to say that if you take any of the medicines he will give you, you will die. I saw Fred K. Smith purchase the medicines he gave you, and saw him put in it enough Strychnine to kill a horse. If you take any of it you will surely die. He is trying to poison you.

Yours truly

H.M.B.

At the request of the police a notice was placed in the window of W.H. Smith's shop in the Strand. Needless to say Mr Bayne failed to 'drop in' and the police were not in the least bit surprised to discover no trace of a barrister of that name.

The borough of Lambeth, and its 'unfortunate women' in particular, had six months of uneasy calm. During this period there were no further incidents but the police made no apparent progress towards catching the cruel murderer of Ellen Donworth. But then, as the arrival of spring began to show even in the most densely inhabited parts of the great city, with house-sparrows building nests and wild flowers daring to grow amongst the bricks and the dirt, it all began again.

At 1.45 a.m. on 12 April 1892, P.C. George Comley, walking his lonely beat, turned into Stamford Street which runs parallel to the river east of Waterloo Station. As he did so, he saw a man come out from number 118 and caught a glimpse of a young woman as she closed the door behind him. Outside number 118 was a street-light and in the dull glow of the gas-flame he was able to see the man clearly. He was about 5' 10" tall, aged forty-five to fifty, clean shaven and wore glasses. He was dressed in a dark overcoat and a high silk hat. After leaving the house he walked away briskly towards Waterloo Road.

Some three quarters of an hour later, when his beat once more brought him into Stamford Street, P.C. Comley was surprised to find more activity at number 118. There was a cab outside and the front door stood wide open, although it was a chilly night with a cold damp wind coming off the river.

Crossing the road, he approached the house, curious to see just what was going on. As he did so another policeman, whom he quickly recognized as his colleague, P.C. William Eversfield, emerged from

38

the building carrying a young woman in his arms. Comley soon learned that the girl's name was Emma Shrivell. The landlord of the house had called the police after being woken by screams coming from the two women tenants on the second floor. Going upstairs to investigate he had found first one girl, then the other, writhing in agony.

Having been told that the second woman, Alice Marsh, was still inside, P.C. Comley went in to fetch her. He found her lying face down over a chair, unconscious. Picking her up in his arms he hurried her to the waiting cab and soon sent it off, rattling noisily on the uneven road, to St Thomas's Hospital. Unfortunately, upon reaching hospital, it was discovered that Alice Marsh was already dead and that her friend was dying. P.C. Comley was able to question Emma Shrivell before she died, however, and she told him that a man had given each of them three pills. She also confirmed that the man responsible was indeed the tall man in the dark overcoat that he had seen being let out at 1.45 a.m.

The doctors at St Thomas's Hospital expressed the opinion that the peculiar symptoms of the girls' poisoning were strongly suggestive of strychnine, although they could not be completely certain until the result of the post-mortem was known.

On the north coast of Devon, far from the smoke and noise of Lambeth, lies the pleasant market-town of Barnstable, looking out over the broad estuary of the River Taw. As nice a spot as you could hope to find. It was here that Dr Joseph Harper practised medicine from his home in Bear Street. His son was in London, studying at St Thomas's Hospital, prior to setting up a practice of his own in the clean air of his native Devon, just across the river at Braughton. At the end of April 1892 Dr Harper received a letter bearing a London post-mark and was astonished at its contents:

Dr Harper, Barnstable.   London April 25th 1892
Dear Sir,
    I am writing to inform you that one of my operatives has indisputable evidence that your son, W.H. Harper, a medical student, of St Thomas's Hospital poisoned two girls named Alice Marsh and Emma Shrivell on the 12th inst. and that I am willing to give you the said evidence (so as you can suppress it) for the sum of £1500 sterling. The evidence in my hands is strong enough to convict and hang your son, but I shall give it to you for £1500 sterling or sell it to the police for the same amount. The publication of the evidence will ruin you and your family for ever and you

know that as well as I do. To show you that what I am writing is
true, I am willing to send you a copy of the evidence against your
son, so that when you read it you will need no one to tell you that
it will convict your son. Answer my letter at once through the
columns of the London *Daily Chronicle* as follows:

'W.H.M. - will pay you for your services. Dr H'

After I see this in the paper I will communicate with you again. As
I said before I am perfectly willing to satisfy you that I have strong
evidence against your son by giving you a copy of it before you pay
me a penny. If you do not answer it at once I am going to give
evidence to the coroner at once.

Yours respectfully,
W.H. Murray

Enclosed with the letter was a collection of newspaper cuttings
relating to the deaths of two women in south London. Understandably, Dr Harper regarded the letter as having been written by some
sort of crank; he had met a few in his long medical career, even in
Devon. He placed the odd document in a drawer of his desk, with the
intention of showing it to his son when they next met.

Inspector Harvey, of the Lambeth police, had seen the last dying
agonies of Ellen Donworth. It was not something that even an
experienced and hardened policeman was likely to forget easily. He
had read the post-mortem report of strychnine poisoning. Now he
had the reports from the two constables, together with the initial
findings from St Thomas's, on Alice Marsh and Emma Shrivell. The
similarities between the cases could not be ignored, nor the
implications - he had a madman on his patch.

Working on the not unreasonable assumption that the man
responsible for the killings might well be living locally, a number of
officers were instructed to make discreet inquiries; not an easy thing
to do in the back streets of Lambeth where the police were not
normally welcomed.

One of those officers was Sergeant Ward. He knew the area well
and was, in turn, well known by its inhabitants. For their part, the
people of Lambeth were more than willing to help. A little burglary,
a bit of receiving, that was one thing, but murder was different - in
this they were at one with the police and gave every co-operation.

Sergeant Ward worked his way round the borough, house by
house, tediously asking the same questions, with little to show for his
efforts but tired feet; until, that is, he reached 88 Lambeth Road.

Here he had a chat with the landlady, Mrs Robertson. In the comfort of her private sitting-room, over the inevitable cup of tea, she told him that the person he should really be speaking to was her new maid, a girl called Lucy Rose.

Lucy was out at the time, it being her half-day off, but later that day Sergeant Ward returned and heard from her a detailed account of the horrid death of Matilda Clover. He did not waste any time in sending his report to Inspector Harvey. The story that Lucy told, particularly her graphic description of those terrible convulsions suffered by Matilda, reminded the inspector all too well of his own observations at the side of the dying Ellen Donworth.

The necessary formal application was made and rapidly granted for the exhumation of the body of Matilda Clover. It took place on 5 May and the long overdue post-mortem was carried out. The results were decisive: strychnine poisoning. Now the police had four known murders on their hands, the post-mortems on Marsh and Shrivell by now having come to the same predictable conclusion.

During the course of the inquest into the deaths of Marsh and Shrivell, the coroner received a letter:

> To the Foreman of the Coroner's Jury in the Case of Alice Marsh and Emma Shrivell.
> Dear Sir,
>   I beg to inform you that one of my operatives has positive proof that Walter Harper, a medical student at St Thomas's Hospital and a son of Dr Harper of Bear St., Barnstable, is responsible for the deaths of Alice Marsh and Emma Shrivell, he having poisoned these girls with strychnine. This is proof you can have on paying my bill for services to George Clarke, detective, Cockspur St. Charing Cross to whom I will give the proof on his paying my bill.
>   Yours respectfully,
>   William H. Murray.

The police quickly visited the offices of Mr Clarke of Cockspur Street, but learned little from him. He ran a perfectly legitimate business and his knowledge of the mysterious W.H. Murray was limited to a strange letter which had turned up in his post:

> George Clarke Esq.   London May 4th 1892
> Dear Sir,
>   If Mr Wyatt, the coroner, calls on you in regard to the murder of Alice Marsh & Emma Shrivell, you can tell him that Walter

Harper, medical student of St Thomas's Hospital and a son of Dr Harper of Bear St. Barnstable, poisoned these girls with strychnine, provided he (the coroner) pays you for your services. I will give the proofs when he comes to terms. I will write you again in a few days.

Yours respectfully,
William H. Murray

In spite of the string of murders that they now believed him to have committed, the police had very little hard evidence capable of leading them to the murderer. They did, however, have at their disposal one man, Police-Constable George Comley, who had seen the killer and who firmly believed that he would recognize him if he saw him again. During the evening of 12 May he did precisely that.

The wanted man was first seen outside the Canterbury Music Hall in Westminster Bridge Road. P.C. Comley, who was luckily in plain clothes at the time, saw him hanging around, looking with obvious interest at any woman who passed him but making no attempt to speak to any of them. Quite soon the constable was joined by Sergeant Ward and together they began carefully to follow their suspect. For a while he just roamed the streets of Lambeth, the two men trying desperately to keep him in sight without themselves being noticed. At last he appeared to tire of his wanderings, turned down into Lambeth Palace Road and, to the relief of his pursuers, entered number 103. Discreet enquiries in the neighbourhood revealed him to be a Dr Thomas Neill.

Meanwhile, on the other side of the river, Detective-Inspector McIntyre of Scotland Yard was having his curiosity aroused. Amongst his wide circle of acquaintances was John Haynes, a man who had, in the past, been useful in various secret but rather minor activities on behalf of the Home Office. Like other men of his type, he often seemed to have a great deal of time on his hands and would occasionally call in on McIntyre for a chat. Often such visits proved to be a waste of time to the busy inspector, but Haynes was observant, had his ear to the ground and, from time to time, produced valuable snippets of information that were difficult to obtain by other means.

Haynes had recently begun to talk of a man called Dr Neill whom he had met at his lodgings in Westminster Bridge Road. His landlord was a Mr Armstead who owned a photographic studio. Dr Neill was originally one of Mr Armstead's customers but had become friendly with the photographer and his wife, frequently having tea with them.

Haynes and Neill also became friendly; soon they were dining together and spending their evenings talking about this and that, as men do. Haynes found his new friend to be an odd man. He claimed to be an agent for an American pharmaceutical company and, for much of the time, talked very much like a professional man. But, at other times, he could be different and Haynes found his way of talking about women quite repellent.

On the morning of 14 May, Haynes, the Armsteads and Dr Neill were all having coffee together at the Armsteads' home when Mrs Armstead commented that a man appeared to be watching the house. Haynes asked Neill, jokingly, if he were the one being watched. To his surprise Neill reacted as if he were taking the suggestion seriously. 'Certainly not,' he declared with some vehemence. When Haynes next visited Scotland Yard he asked Inspector McIntyre whether they were watching Neill. He received a non-committal answer.

The following day Haynes and Neill once more had lunch together. During the course of the meal Haynes, his curiosity having been aroused, broached the topic of the man who had been watching the Armsteads' house. He was rewarded when Neill confessed that the police were indeed watching him. It was, he said, a case of mistaken identity. They thought that he was a man called Harper, with whom he shared lodgings. He then gave a long, extraordinarily rambling account of how Harper killed the two girls in Stamford Street because they were trying to blackmail him. Then, clearly excited by Haynes's obvious eagerness to hear more, he went on to claim that not only had Harper killed Marsh and Shrivell, but other girls, Clover, Donworth and Harvey.

Haynes, like everyone else in the area, was by now all too familiar with four of these names but who, he asked, was Harvey? Louise Harvey was a girl who died outside the Oxford Music Hall, he was told. Clearly flattered at having such an eager and attentive audience, Neill offered to show Haynes where the girl had lived in St John's Wood. Haynes, by no means sure whether or not his companion was making it up as he went along, readily agreed to this suggestion.

Neill led him first to Lambeth Road and showed him where Matilda Clover had lived and died. Then they travelled to St John's Wood, to 55 Townsend Road. 'That was where she lived,' Neill said, and invited Haynes to question the occupants. When Haynes attempted to do so, however, the woman who opened the door denied ever having heard of Louise Harvey and, since she was clearly viewing them with growing suspicion, they chose to withdraw. On their way back to the centre of London, Haynes asked Neill why he didn't tell the police all he knew about the case. 'There's more to be made down at Barnstable,' was the reply he was given.

Not many hours passed before Haynes was once more in Scotland Yard, relating the whole curious story to his friend, Detective-Inspector McIntyre. Following the previous visit of Haynes, the inspector had been to see his colleagues across the river in Lambeth and by now knew all about their suspicions of Dr Thomas Neill.

It must be born in mind that, up until now, the Lambeth hunt for a murderer and the Scotland Yard search for a blackmailer had been carried out in total ignorance of each other's activities. Now this unfortunate state of affairs had ended. The Lambeth police were able to confirm to their colleagues across the river that they had had Neill under continuous observation ever since his identification by P.C. Comley. In return, Scotland Yard were able to tell them about the blackmail letters.

In response to the latest story from Haynes, Inspector McIntyre decided that he would very much like to meet this curious Dr Neill. It was not too difficult to arrange, he 'just happened' to bump into him at the Armsteads' house. He was very experienced at getting men to feel at ease and to talk freely to him. Soon Neill was telling the sympathetic inspector all about the wicked Harper and the stupid Lambeth police who were harassing him.

Quite soon a meeting was arranged at a convenient public-house; this included not only Neill and McIntyre, but also Chief-Inspector Mulvaney of Scotland Yard and Inspector Harvey from Lambeth. The meeting was ostensibly to discuss Neill's complaint of being watched. He told them that he had been questioned at some length by a detective named Murray who wanted to know all about Harper whom he had described as a murder suspect. None of the police officers present had ever heard of a detective called Murray and, in spite of all their subsequent efforts, they were unable to trace any such officer.

Attempts were made to investigate the alleged murder of Louise Harvey but they quickly ran into a series of brick walls. Enquiries in St John's Wood disclosed that a Louise Harvey had indeed lived in Townsend Road, but at number 44, not number 55 and no one knew where she had gone. This would only be expected had she been murdered, but they could find no evidence that she had been. Indeed, they could find no evidence that she had died at all. She had quite simply vanished. But, as a direct result of the press coverage on the inquest of Emma Shrivell and Alice Marsh, a young woman came forward with a remarkable story.

She gave her name as Louise Harris but said that, in October 1891, she had been calling herself Louise Harvey. This was because, at that time, she had been living with a man named Charles Harvey in St John's Wood.

One evening she was approached by a man at the Alhambra. Later that same evening she met him again outside St James's Hall and they spent the night together at an hotel in Berwick Street, Soho. He told her that he was a doctor from St Thomas's Hospital and came from America. The next morning, before leaving her, he commented on some spots that she had on her forehead and said that he could get something for her that would get rid of them. They agreed to meet again on the embankment near Charing Cross Station.

Louise was far from happy about the talk of medicines and told Charles Harvey the story. As a result, when she went to meet the man again, Harvey was close at hand watching and ready to intervene should it prove necessary. Louise was rather late for the appointment but the man seemed not to mind. He suggested going to a music hall and asked her which she would prefer. She chose the Oxford. He was perfectly agreeable to this but suggested that, as he had brought the promised medicine for her spots and they needed to be taken after a drink, they should go first to the Northumberland public-house. Here she had a glass of wine and, upon leaving, he bought her some roses. He also purchased some figs for her to take after the medicine.

The man now explained, with regret, that he would not be able to go with her to the music hall after all. He had to keep an important appointment at St Thomas's. He would, however, give her the money for her ticket and they could meet outside the theatre afterwards.

At this point he produced from his pocket two pills wrapped in tissue paper. They were long and tapered and he told her that they must be swallowed whole, not bitten. Louise was both far too frightened and far too sensible to take them. He placed the two pills in her right hand. She raised it to her mouth and pretended to swallow. He then made her show him her right hand and she did so. It was empty. She had to allow him to look into her mouth; it too was empty. The pills were, in fact, now in her left hand and at the earliest opportunity she threw them away. He seemed to be very pleased with her, said she was a good, sensible girl, gave her 5s. for the music hall and wanted to call her a cab. This offer she declined, saying that she would soon find one in the Strand.

As soon as he was gone she was quickly joined by Charles Harvey, who had been hovering nearby, and she related everything that had taken place. They then went to the Oxford together. When they emerged at about eleven, they looked around for the strange doctor but there was no sign of him.

A week or so later she saw him again, but he seemed not to recognize her and asked her name. When told that it was Harvey and that they had had an arrangement to meet outside the Oxford, he turned abruptly and walked away.

As a result of the meeting between Detective-Inspector McIntyre and Neill, during the course of which the police had obtained a sample of the doctor's handwriting, Scotland Yard appointed Detective-Inspector Tonbridge to take overall command of the case.

Using the complaint of police harassment as an excuse, the inspector paid a visit to 103 Lambeth Palace Road, intending to question Neill. But he was in for a surprise. Neill was not alone, he had his fiancée with him and Inspector Tonbridge was soon being introduced to Miss Laura Sabatini. He was taken aback, Miss Sabatini was charming, attractive and demure. This was clearly not the time to discuss the cruel murder of prostitutes. He did, however, manage to question Neill about his occupation as salesman and ask to see his trade samples. They were kept in a neat, businesslike case and included a large quantity of strychnine. When asked about it, Neill assured him that he only sold to chemists, never to the general public.

As part of his investigation, Inspector Tonbridge had the files searched and questions asked for any letters which might conceivably be relevant to the case. Five came to light, one to Dr Broadbent, one to Mr F. Smith, two to the Surrey coroner and one to the private detective, Mr Clarke. A careful comparison of signatures and handwriting was made. The letters to Dr Broadbent and to Mr F. Smith were quite clearly in the distinctive handwriting of Dr Thomas Neill.

On 1 June Inspector Tonbridge travelled to Devon where he interviewed the young and recently qualified Dr Harper who was busy establishing his own practice. The young man was totally straightforward and soon told the inspector about the odd letter that his father had received from London. They crossed the long Taw bridge together and made their way to the home of the elder Dr

Harper. A few minutes later the letter was in the inspector's hand. It did not need an expert to tell him that the handwriting was that of Dr Neill. He returned to London triumphant; the long train journey had been well worthwhile.

Two days later, on the afternoon of 3 June, Detective-Inspector Tonbridge stopped Neill in the street and arrested him on a charge of attempting to blackmail Dr Harper. Later, when formally charged, he asked for his solicitor. He was offered a telegraph form. 'I write nothing,' he said. 'You send it for me.'

With Neill safely deposited in Holloway Prison, the police were able to investigate him more freely, beginning with his lodgings. They heard from his landlady's daughter that, after the death of Matilda Clover, he had told her that a friend of his had died suddenly in Lambeth Road. He said that he suspected that she had been poisoned and asked the girl to make enquiries on his behalf. This she had resolutely refused to do. Some time later he told her, 'I know who poisoned the woman in Lambeth Road. It was Earl Russell.'

It was about that time that Lady Russell received a letter saying that the writer could help her obtain a divorce if she so wished. It also said that he could hang Lord Russell because of evidence that Lord Russell had poisoned a woman called Clover at 27 South Lambeth Road. Lady Russell, like most people in the public eye, was used to letters from cranks and paid little attention to it. In any case she was at the time trying to obtain a divorce on the grounds of her husband's homosexual behaviour, so that the alleged murder of a prostitute would not have been much help to her.

The police were also told that, on Easter Sunday 1892, while she was dusting the room of one of the other lodgers, Neill's landlady had been interrupted by Neill coming into the room and asking a great many questions about the occupant. What was his name? Where did he come from? Who was his father? The other lodger involved was Dr Harper.

Enquiries slightly further afield took the police to the chemist's shop at 22 Parliament Street, run by a Mr Benjamin Priest. In the middle of October 1891 Mr Priest received a visit from a new customer, a tall, broad-shouldered man with glasses and a heavy moustache. He asked the proprietor for an ounce of 'nux vomica', a mixture of morphine and strychnine. This, being an extremely dangerous poison, was on the restricted list. The customer, who gave his name as Thomas Neill, explained, however, that he was a doctor attached to St Thomas's Hospital, just across the river. This Mr

Priest considered to be a perfectly adequate explanation and supplied his visitor with the requested drugs.

On subsequent occasions he supplied the man with further quantities of the poison and also obtained for him boxes of empty drug capsules. After the customer's first visit Mr Priest had checked in the Medical Register but accounted for the complete absence of a Dr Thomas Neill as the result of the man's obvious American accent.

One person, completely shattered by the arrest of Dr Neill, was Miss Laura Sabatini of Chapel Street, Berkhamsted. A small, quiet, elegant woman of thirty, she first met Neill in November 1891. They became friendly, dined and attended concerts together. Laura lived with her mother, worked as a dressmaker and had a quiet, sheltered, rather lonely life, giving her little contact with men. Dr Neill was kind, attentive and considerate, the perfect gentleman. Before long she found herself engaged to him. Her mother thought him rather odd but, having almost given up hope that her daughter would marry, saw no reason to interfere.

Early in December Neill suddenly announced to Laura that he was proposing to return to America to settle his financial affairs. Upon his return, he said, they would marry. Prior to his departure he gave her a copy of a will which, he said, he had made out in her favour. He explained that he had left all his property to her and that it was impossible for him to make another will. This was, of course, complete nonsense.

When he returned from America in April 1892 they resumed their relationship. On 2 May he asked her to write some letters for him. She wondered why he could not write them himself but, when she queried it, he gave no reply. He had previously given hints to her about having done secret work for the government, so she thought it best not to press the matter. The letters were then written, by her, to his dictation. One letter was to the county coroner accusing Mr Harper of the murders of Alice Marsh and Emma Shrivell. Another was to Mr Clarke, a private enquiry agent. Both letters were signed W.H. Murray. Miss Sabatini asked Neill if he really knew anything about the murders and was told that he had a detective friend who was employed on the case.

Amongst Neill's personal possessions, the police found a small notebook. Inside was a list of the murdered girls' initials, together with the dates of their deaths. The list included Louise Harvey.

Scotland Yard soon learnt that the man calling himself Thomas Neill was, in fact, Thomas Neill Cream and gradually, with the assistance of the authorities in Canada and the United States, they were able to piece together the life of this strange, mentally unbalanced man.

He had been born in Glasgow but, while still very young, his parents had chosen to emigrate first to America and then to Canada. For a short while he joined his father's business but soon developed a passionate interest in medicine. Encouraged by his father he was sent to McGill College, Montreal. His studies lasted from 1872 until 1876 and it was then that he first obtained a degree.

Soon afterwards he travelled to England and attended lectures at St Thomas's Hospital with the intention of obtaining an MRCS degree. This, however, he failed to do. He moved to Edinburgh and it was there, after a further period of study, that he obtained the necessary degree and became a qualified surgeon. In doing so he apparently impressed his examiners with the extent of his medical knowledge.

After qualifying he returned to Canada where he practised for a short time in Ontario. But, as a result of having been implicated in a case of illegal abortion, he had to leave Canada hurriedly and moved across the border to Chicago. Soon he once more involved himself in an illegal abortion and was very lucky to avoid imprisonment.

Only a year later, in 1880, he seduced one of his own patients and killed her husband with strychnine. The man's death was at first declared to be from natural causes, but Cream's fondness for reading about his crimes and for blaming them on others was already developing. He wrote, firstly, to the coroner and then to the District Attorney, accusing the chemist, who had supplied the man's medicine, of negligence. This led first to a post-mortem and then to the arrest, not of the chemist but of Cream. For this he was sentenced to life imprisonment. This was reduced, on appeal, to seventeen years and, after eleven years in an American prison, he was released to inflict his murderous epidemic on Lambeth.

Immediately after his release from prison in the early autumn of 1891, he sailed for England, arriving at Liverpool at the beginning of October. Taking the first available train he travelled to London where he booked into Anderton's Hotel in Fleet Street. He stayed there, however, for only a few days before he found lodgings at 103 Lambeth Palace Road on 7 October. From the moment of his arrival in England he became Dr Thomas Neill.

During the period of his American imprisonment his father had died, leaving him relatively well off and able to indulge freely in his tastes for women and cruel murder. While he had a more than adequate income, however, the capital remained in the control of trustees. It was with the intention of loosening their hold on his financial affairs, using his forthcoming marriage to Miss Sabatini as an excuse, that he made his journey across the Atlantic in the winter of 1891.

At his eventual trial, at the Old Bailey before Mr Justice Hawkins, the outcome was certain, defence counsel taking the only possible line of defence – Cream was insane. That, however, was not the immediate concern of the jury and they were able to fulfil their function in only twelve minutes with a verdict of 'Guilty'.

In sentencing the man to death, specifically for the murder of Matilda Clover, Mr Justice Hawkins made his own opinion perfectly clear:

> Thomas Neill, the jury, after having listened to the evidence which has been offered against you in respect of the most terrible crime and having paid all attention to the most able arguments and the very eloquent speech which your learned counsel addressed to them on your behalf, have felt it their bounden duty to find you guilty of the crime of wilful murder. That murder was so diabolical in its character, fraught with so much cold-blooded cruelty, that one dare hardly trust oneself to speak of the details of your wickedness.
>
> What motive could have actuated you to take the life of that poor girl away, and with so much torture to that poor creature, who could not have offended you, I know not. But I do know that your cruelty towards her, and the crime that you committed are to my mind of unparalleled atrocity. For the crime of which you have been convicted our laws know but one penalty – the penalty of death.

The next day the *Daily Chronicle* wrote its own epitaph:

> His wickedness is thus a horrible combination of sordid greed, of low cunning, ruthless brutality and fiendish cruelty. The records of the Central Criminal Court have never displayed a more disgusting figure than his, lurking for his prey in the dark and dirty holes and corners of a great sin-stricken city and projecting its loathsome shadow over our depraved social system.

As he stood upon the scaffold, blind-folded, with the trap-door beneath his feet, Cream is reputed to have uttered his last words, 'I am Jack the R—.'

From time to time, amongst the seemingly endless conjecture as to the identity of the Ripper, the name of Thomas Neill Cream is offered as a serious suspect. After all, he did murder prostitutes and he was a qualified surgeon. This does, however, ignore one small, irrefutable fact; at the time of the Ripper killings Cream was safely locked away in a Chicago prison cell, an unbreakable alibi if ever there was one.

The question that has to be asked about Thomas Neill Cream is this: was he really sane?

The authorities at the time considered the matter and came to the conclusion that he was sane, that the motive for his crimes was attempted blackmail, that he poisoned his victims with the deliberate intention of accusing other men and demanding money for his silence. But this argument is difficult to sustain. While it is perfectly true that, after each crime he sent demands for money, they were hardly realistic.

Firstly, Cream was an educated man. If he were sane he must have known perfectly well that respectable men like Frederick Smith or Dr Broadbent could not really be expected to pay over large sums of money in such circumstances. For blackmail to stand any chance of success there has to be at least some vestige of truth, however tenuous, in the allegation. It is highly unlikely that there was any connection whatever between his murder victims and the recipients of his attempted blackmail demands.

Secondly, although he sent financial demands he never seems to have made any attempt to follow them up. Even in cases like that of Dr Broadbent, when the police entered the requested message in the newspaper, he made no attempt to take the bait.

And thirdly, the sums of money demanded were frequently so enormous as to be ridiculous: the offer to the Surrey coroner of assistance in exchange for £300,000, for instance, or the £1500 demanded from Dr Harper, a figure far beyond the means of a country doctor.

If we exclude blackmail, what other motive was there for his actions? None of the women had ever done him any harm or were in any position to do so. He hardly knew them. The sole motive was for the sheer pleasure of inflicting the maximum amount of pain; of killing in the cruellest way possible. The blackmail letters were just another manifestation of that same urge, the infliction of mental cruelty.

Unfortunately, as we are all well aware, it is perfectly possible to enjoy cruelty without being insane, but reading of Cream's behaviour it is difficult not to believe that he suffered from some serious mental derangement.

There was one postscript to the case. Laura Sabatini, tired of expressions of incredulity from other women as to how she could have contemplated marrying such an obvious monster, released a letter to the press. A letter written to her by Cream. It is a quite remarkable document which only serves to increase the mystery of the character of a decidedly peculiar man.

> Miss Laura Sabatini   London. Dec. 1st 1891
> Dearest Laura,
>
> I have just received your favour of yesterdays date, in which you convey to me the joyful news that you have given my proposal of marriage favourable consideration and the assurance that you will become my loving little wife, just as soon as I return from America, after having finished my business there. The receipt of your letter has brought me a pleasure in my life that I have never before felt. May the Giver of all good reward you my darling for the great happiness you have brought into my life, for I know not how to do so! I shall, however, my darling, give you all the care and all the kindness that a fond, loving and devoted husband can give. I shall devote all my life, my Laura, to your future happiness, and all I ask in return is your love, my little darling. Give me this, dearest, and I shall be as faithful, loyal, constant and true to you as God ever made a man. Surely I am not asking too much, my love, for a life-long devotion? I shall get you your engagement-ring as soon as I get my draft from America. After I get settled with my father's estate, I shall provide you with a life annuity of £100 (One hundred pounds) a year, so that in the event of misfortune happening to me it will never hurt you. I shall make my will in your favour and will carry all the insurance on my life that my little income will permit me to do. Beyond this I can offer you nothing but the truest of love and genuine devotion. It is a small reward for the great happiness you have brought me, but it is the best that I can do, and more than most men give their wives. I lay this offering now at the feet of my love, with a request that she will take the best care of herself till I return; then I will do the rest.
>
>   Yours with love for ever,
>   T. Neill Cream.

THE BROKEN LANTERN

THE BROKEN
LANTERN

L et us make no bones about it, Albert Milsom was a crook. A professional criminal. He would think nothing of forcing entry into your house and violating the sanctity of your home. He would happily steal your most treasured possessions and sell for trivial sums items of irreplaceable, sentimental value. Old-fashioned moralists would have said of him that he would be bound to come to a bad end. And they would have been right. He did.

About the only good thing that could be said about Albert Milsom was that, in spite of his powerful build, he was not by nature a violent man. By February 1896, when he was thirty-two years old, he had behind him a long criminal history, usually for burglary. The police knew him under a number of names: Albert Milsom, Charles Wilson, James Mead and Charles Smith. About 5' 6" tall he had a dark complexion, dark-brown hair, hazel eyes and, if asked his occupation, would have said 'stoker'. With his twenty-five-year-old wife Emily and their two small children he lived with his wife's mother at 133 Southam Street in what was then known as Kensal Town. Also living in the house was his wife's brother, Henry Miller, a lad of fifteen.

Milsom developed a long association with another resident of Kensal Town, Henry Fowler. He, too, had a long criminal record and a similar fondness for aliases: Henry Fowler, Henry Sabard, Thomas Brown. He was usually known to his friends as 'Bunny'. Taller than Milsom, he was 5' 10", had dark hair, brown eyes and a mole on the left side of his nose. He described himself as a billiard-marker. Fowler, like Milsom, was a burglar. The big difference between them was that Fowler was a dangerously violent man. On 16 January 1896 he came out of prison, on parole, after serving a sentence for burglary with violence. Both men, though they appear to have been curiously unaware of it, were of continuing interest to the police.

Within a few weeks of Fowler's release from Dartmoor the two men were once more associating. Fowler made frequent visits to Southam Street and occasionally they went out together late at night and did not return until the early morning. Neither of them appeared to have an honest occupation.

At about eight o'clock on the evening of 13 February Fowler turned up at Milsom's home and put a suggestion to him.

> I have had a look round with another man who done a lagging with me, and he pointed out several places. There is one place especially where an old man lives. You know how them people are. Any little hole or corner they put their money in. We might find something there. Will you come?

According to Milsom he, himself, was reluctant and it took Fowler a considerable time to persuade him to take part. Given his record, however, it seems unlikely that he took too much persuading. At any rate he agreed. Fowler asked for 'a bit of candle' but was told that none was available. He then looked around the room and saw a small lantern on the kitchen dresser. It had three glasses, white, green and red, similar to those used by railway guards.

'That belongs to my little brother-in-law,' said Milsom.

'We will take that, it won't throw the reflection so,' replied Fowler.

The two men went first to Kilburn where they entered a public-house and met up with three or four of Fowler's friends, including some who had only just emerged from Dartmoor. He asked them the best way to get to Muswell Hill. After a few drinks they walked to the nearest tube-station and travelled to north London where they went into another public-house for a few more drinks. It being then sufficiently late for business, they set off for their planned target, Muswell Lodge, Tetherdown, the home of Mr Henry Smith.

Muswell Lodge was a large house, standing in its own extensive grounds. The main entrance, protected by a high gate, was in Tetherdown Lane. At the rear were large gardens stretching down to Coldfell Woods.

Mr Henry Smith, who was seventy-nine but strong and vigorous for his age, lived alone, having been a widower for twenty-four years.

He was very security conscious, everywhere was always carefully locked at night and there was an alarm-gun protecting the rear of the premises from any possible incursion from the woods. This comprised a gun linked to a wire which stretched across the full width of the garden. A series of iron staves kept the wire in position about 18" above the ground. Anyone touching the wire would fire the alarm-gun.

Charles Webber of 1 Coppets Road had been employed by Mr Smith, as a gardener, for ten years. In the winter months he started work as soon as it became light and left at 5.30 p.m. On Thursday, 13 February, he left the garden as usual, after setting the alarm-gun. At 11.30 p.m. he returned to bank up the greenhouse fire, letting himself in and out by the side gate. Mr Smith always went to bed by eight o'clock. All seemed quiet and secure.

When the two burglars reached the house, Fowler climbed the front gate with Milsom close behind. Fowler warned his companion to beware of electric alarms or, he said, 'we shall find ourselves surrounded by police'. They made their way round the back of the building to where there was a large lawn with a group of shrubs in the centre. Here they lay down and waited, watching and listening for any sound from the house. They had been there motionless for almost an hour before Fowler suddenly whispered. 'We will get to work.'

Moving quietly up to the house they began to search for a way in. It was by no means easy. The drawing-room window was tried first. Carefully, Fowler forced his jemmy under the sash and gradually brought his full strength to bear but, in spite of all his efforts, it refused to yield. They next tried a small scullery window but it proved to be securely barred. Moving further on, they came across another window. Carefully removing flowerpots which stood on the sill, Fowler forced a chisel under the window, heaved and felt it give way. Sliding up the sash he climbed inside.

It appeared to be a small kitchen. He moved silently to the door which led to the rest of the house and turned the handle. It was locked. He opened his bag and removed a drill-brace and bit. Within a few moments he was at work drilling holes around the door lock. What he did not know, however, was that Henry Smith slept in the room immediately above the kitchen. Fowler successfully drilled two holes in the door and was about to start on the third when Milsom hissed a warning. A light was showing under the door, growing steadily in strength. Someone was coming down the stairs. Milsom called, 'Bunny, out you come, there's someone coming,' but Fowler made no attempt to leave through the window. There was the sound of a key being inserted in the lock, a loud 'click' as it turned and then the door began, slowly, very cautiously to open.

At this point, if we are to believe Milsom, he panicked and ran for the gate and safety, expecting Fowler to be close at his heels. Instead he heard shouts of 'Police! Murder!' He stood nervously by the gate, watching the street anxiously for lights or sounds of movement, but there were none. It seemed to him quite inconceivable that no one had heard the sounds from the house, but that clearly was the case. Gradually recovering his nerve he slowly returned to the now silent house. Fowler stood by the back door. He was covered in blood; it was on his face, his coat, his hands. But the blood was not his own.

Milsom, horrified, gasped, 'Good God, Fowler, what have you done?' The reply was fierce. 'It's outing dues,' snarled Fowler, 'and all through you, you cur, for leaving a man on his own.' For a few moments it seemed possible that Fowler, who was still wildly angry, would turn his violence on Milsom, but he gradually calmed down. 'Oh well,' he said, 'it's no use crying. Stop there, I'll go upstairs and see if I can find any money.'

Milsom did as he was told and, after some time, his associate returned with a watch and chain and some items of jewellery. 'I have found the Peter,' he said, meaning the safe, 'and the key in the old man's trousers. I won't take the jewellery in case of detection.' Fowler then washed the blood off his hands in the kitchen and wiped his coat with a towel.

Leaving the house, the two men returned to the shrubbery where they buried their tools: brace and bit, chisel and screwdriver. After waiting a few minutes to make sure that no one was about, they clambered over the back fence and escaped into the trees. Creeping about in the dark, damp woods, they soon found a tree-stump and sat down to wait. Because of the danger of being stopped by police patrols, in which case Fowler's blood-stained clothing would soon be spotted, it would not be safe for them to move before dawn.

They sat there, amongst the bare trees and the thick dead leaves, for three or four hours and then made their way back towards the road. They emerged from the woods at about six o'clock and found themselves once more in Tetherdown Lane, although well away from the house. The two men then set off on the long weary walk to Kensal Town with Fowler wearing Milsom's coat to hide his clothing. When, at last, they were almost home Fowler announced that he would go to his brother's place for breakfast and told Milsom that he would see him in a couple of hours. Milsom, by no means sorry to lose his companion, went quickly to Southam Street which he reached at about seven o'clock. He immediately went to bed, totally exhausted from his night's work.

While Milsom and Fowler had been tramping the long way back to Kensal, Charles Webber was on his way to work. Mr Smith was normally a very early riser and would usually unlock the front gate before the gardener arrived. Webber was therefore surprised to find it still locked. Letting himself in, he went round to the garden. He soon discovered that the alarm-gun had been tampered with, the wire having been removed from the two centre supports. With increasing concern he went to the house and knocked on the front door. There was no reply. Going once more to the back of the building he looked through the kitchen window. Something was lying on the floor, but he was unable to see precisely what it was.

By now very worried, Mr Webber decided to go for assistance. He went first to Joseph Stanbrook, a nurseryman of 3 Tetherdown. The rest of the neighbourhood was now beginning to awaken to another day and, seeing unusual activity at Muswell Lodge, they soon came to investigate. But still nothing constructive seems to have been done until the arrival on the scene of Major George Challen, retired Major of Volunteers. At least that was the opinion of the Major. Suitably armed, he was soon leading Webber and Stanbrook up the drive and round to the rear of the premises. The kitchen window was shut and the blind down. Peering under the blind he saw a body lying on the floor.

Getting into the house proved to be all too easy; the kitchen door, normally locked and bolted, opened at the first touch. With the intrepid Major leading the way the three men entered the kitchen. They saw Henry Smith immediately. He lay on the floor, on his back, with his head under the corner of the kitchen sink. He was partly covered by a red tablecloth.

Dressed in a white night-shirt, he had been bound hand and foot, his arms and hands by a torn-up tablecloth, his ankles by a duster. A towel had been forced into his mouth. There were bruises and wounds on his head and hands. Major Challen cut some of his bonds but it was all too obvious that he had been dead for some time. They could do nothing but send for the police.

When the law officers arrived they immediately began a thorough search of the house and garden. They soon discovered that the burglars had made two previous attempts to break into the house before successfully forcing entry through the back kitchen window by means of a jemmy. The kitchen showed all the signs of a desperate struggle. There were two separate pools of blood on the floor and splashes of blood on the walls. The kitchen fire had been laid but not lit. On the table was a drill-brace. An empty money-bag lay on the floor and, lying in the sink, they came across a curious small, broken lantern with multi-coloured glasses.

Moving into the pantry, the police found a small basket containing a gold watch and chain, together with a pair of spectacles, a number of rings, breast-pins, brooches and similar small items of jewellery. Proceeding upstairs they discovered, in a bedroom, an iron safe, open and empty except for a small family photograph. A deed-box lay on the floor. It too had been rifled, its contents strewn about the floor. These seemed to comprise share certificates and a Post Office savings book, although there was also a wedding ring and some Maundy coins. The bed-clothes were in a heap on the middle of the bed as if someone had hurriedly searched beneath the mattress.

Turning their attention to the garden they discovered a tobacco box which Mr Webber assured them belonged neither to him nor to Henry Smith. The footprints of two men, leading to marks on the high fence at the bottom of the garden, clearly showed the burglars' escape route. Beyond the fence lay Coldfell Woods.

A post-mortem on the unfortunate Henry Smith revealed that, for his age, he had been a remarkably fit man. Six feet tall, weighing seventeen stone and powerfully built, he had clearly put up a tremendous fight. He had a black eye, about a dozen scalp wounds, cuts on both hands and one of his fingers was broken. His skull was fractured. It seemed likely that his assailant had beaten him about the head with a jemmy. Death had been caused by concussion and loss of blood.

Meanwhile, at ten o'clock that same Friday morning, Fowler turned up once again at Southam Street. Under his arm he carried a parcel containing new clothes. At his request Emily Milsom left the room so that he could change into them. He then gave Milsom £50 saying, 'That's more than some would give you after leaving a man in a hole.' Milsom took the money without comment. Fowler then asked, 'Ain't you going to buy new clothes?' to which Milsom replied, 'There's plenty of time for that.' Shortly afterwards Fowler left, leaving his old clothes behind for Emily Milsom to dispose of.

On Saturday, Albert Milsom went out with his wife, Emily, and her young brother Henry Miller. He took them to Harrow Road where he bought some new clothes – a black overcoat, jacket, waistcoat and striped trousers. He paid in gold. Young Henry carried the clothes home but not before he and his sister had visited other shops to buy new clothes for her. Upon returning home Milsom changed into his new clothes which now included a pair of brown boots. Some of his old clothes he gave to Henry.

At about six o'clock that Saturday evening Fowler returned. He now wore a ring on his finger and sported a watch-chain, but without having a watch attached to it. He said that he had been to see some friends who had just come home from 'penal'. He stayed and had tea with the Milsoms.

That evening Mr and Mrs Milsom, together with Fowler and a lady-friend of his, went over to Kilburn to a public-house where there was a concert. They remained there until 12.30, by which time Fowler was very much the worse for drink and becoming violent. He began to quarrel with his girl, punching her and knocking her down. Milsom obtained a cab and, not without difficulty, succeeded in getting Fowler and the girl into it. All four of them then returned in the cab to Southam Street where they parted.

Henry Miller, who had noticed the disappearance of his lantern and had begun to ask awkward questions about it, was told by Milsom, 'If anybody asks you about the lantern you are to say you broke it and threw it in the dust-hole. It pretty nigh caught us in the fire.'

On Sunday, 16 February, Milsom went out in the morning saying that he would be back to dinner, but failed to return. He had gone to meet Fowler who told him, 'I'm off. I have got to show myself on the 16th and I don't intend to give my face away.' This referred to the fact that he was out on licence, was required to report to the police once a month and that month was now up. Milsom asked him where he intended to go. Fowler thought for a moment and then said, 'Will you come abroad?' Milsom, who had never been out of the country in his life but had often thought that he would like to, replied, 'Yes.'

As they suspected, with good reason, that the police might already be on their trail, they took measures to prevent themselves from being followed. They first walked to Kilburn where they caught a cab to Edgware Road and then changed to another cab which took them to Mile End. From there Milsom led Fowler through a maze of narrow East End streets to see his aunt, Mrs Waddell, at 62 St Peter's Street. He introduced Fowler to his aunt as Mr Jarvis.

The two men stayed to dinner. During the course of conversation Milsom told his aunt that the reason that he had come to see her was to say 'goodbye' as he was about to go abroad. Later that evening they went out for a drink with Milsom's cousin, Jack Waddell, and while they were drinking Milsom asked him to get some paper, an envelope and a stamp. These items having been obtained, he wrote a letter to his mother telling her of his plans. He asked her to meet him the next day, bringing his wife and children with her. Before going out that evening both men handed their loaded revolvers to Jack Waddell with the request that he put them in a safe place. Returning to St Peter's Street they stayed the night, sharing a bed with cousin Jack.

On Monday, as planned, Milsom's parents, together with his wife and children, all came to his aunt's house at Mile End. After they had been together for a couple of hours, Milsom rose and said, 'Well, I must be off.' His aunt asked, 'Would you like your wife to come a little way with you? We will mind the children.' Taking up this kind offer the two men, together with Emily Milsom, made their way to Mile End station, but not before retrieving their revolvers.

Once there, they made enquiries as to the next train for Liverpool. They soon learned that they would have a long wait at Mile End for a train and that it would be necessary for them to change. They would almost certainly, as a result, lose their connecting train. Accordingly, they left the station and hailed a cab to take them directly to Euston. Before entering the cab, Milsom said goodbye to his wife and promised to write as soon as possible. They reached Euston just in time to catch the Liverpool train and by late evening were safely on Merseyside.

The flight to Liverpool was not a moment too soon. Police investigations were leading inexorably towards Milsom and Fowler. A plain-clothes detective in the North Kensington force, P.C. Burrell, had been directed to keep an eye on Fowler almost as soon as his release from Dartmoor in January. Fowler's association with Milsom, also a known criminal, had not gone unnoticed. Their sudden ostentatious affluence on 15 February was highly suspicious and its coincidental timing with the Muswell Hill murder soon noted. Their subsequent disappearance and Fowler's failure to report on the 16th, rapidly brought the police baying at their heels.

Milsom and Fowler were meanwhile settling down in Liverpool. Having found suitable lodgings. Milsom wrote to his wife to let her know where he was. By return, he received a telegram from her saying that his brother Fred would be coming to Liverpool the next day. Upon his arrival Fred handed Milsom a sealed letter from his wife:

Dear Albert,

The police have been down here asking where you are. They know you are along with Fowler and you'll get twelve months for being in his company as he is wanted on his licence.

Fred stayed the night in Liverpool, before returning to London the next day. The two fugitives remained in Liverpool for over a week, during which time Fowler went to a dentist and had some false teeth fitted. He was apparently aware that the official police description mentioned that he had some front teeth missing.

Police enquiries had by this time unearthed the fact that two men answering the description of Milsom and Fowler had been seen at Euston. They were wearing new clothes and new brown boots, but had no luggage except for small brown-paper parcels. The police now made a second visit to Southam Street and had a long talk with fifteen-year-old Henry Miller, Milsom's brother-in-law, about the small broken lantern found at Muswell Lodge. Henry told them the truth.

Having been shown the lantern, he confirmed immediately that it was, indeed, his. He told them he had bought it in the Post Office in Golborne Road shortly before Christmas. When purchased it did not work properly. He had repaired it himself and those repairs were still clearly visible. He had inserted a small piece of brass on the burner to keep the wick from the oil. As it had had no wick, he had made one from a small piece of flannelette that his sister had been using to make a shirt. He had also rubbed the glass with sandpaper to remove some spots of varnish which had splashed onto it. All of these easily checked facts meant that the lantern had certainly been the one from the Milsom household.

The lad also told them that the lantern had stood on the kitchen dresser and that it had disappeared on the very night of the Muswell Hill burglary. In addition, he revealed that that same night Milsom did not return home until the early hours, waking young Henry in the process. When Chief-Inspector Marshall conducted a thorough search of 133 Southam Street he found pawn-tickets in a teapot on the dresser. The police went to the relevent pawn-broker, a Mr Harvey, and recovered a bundle of clothing. It included a jacket, a waistcoat, a pair of trousers and a damaged felt hat. The jacket still showed blood-stains.

The police now knew without any doubt that they were on the track of Henry Smith's murderers. As their drag-net closed in on Liverpool, the two fugitives were saved by Fowler's fondness for causing trouble and drawing attention to himself. One evening he took a woman back to his room. This caused a row with their landlady and ended with them being thrown out of their lodgings. They spent one night in an hotel and the next day moved on to Cardiff. Whether by this time the idea of going abroad had been abandoned, or whether they thought that it might be easier to escape from the country via the port of Cardiff rather than Liverpool, is something upon which we can only speculate. What is certain is that, by suddenly changing their locale, they succeeded, more by luck than judgement, in throwing the police off their tracks for some time.

At that period Cardiff was an ideal place for a man on the run. One of the busiest ports in the country and completely cosmopolitan in the port area. Tiger Bay was not a place where sensible people asked too many awkward questions.

Soon after their arrival they went to visit Madame D'Arc's Waxworks Show in St Mary Street. In addition to the waxworks exhibition they found an extra attraction. Not long before, Professor Sinclair, the Eminent Phrenologist (his own description), had written to Madame D'Arc, the proprietress of the waxworks, offering his services.

Writing from Salford, the Professor did not exhibit any false modesty. He assured her that his mere presence would bring vast crowds flocking to her establishment and that his skills would amaze the entire city. As if that were not enough, his wife had a quite remarkable mind-reading and second-sight act. Madame D'Arc had been in the business too long to be over-impressed by fulsome self-praise, but considered that she had little to lose by giving them a trial. She therefore booked them for a month.

Milsom and Fowler paid for a private consultation with the Professor and had the bumps on their heads read. In the circumstances this was a somewhat curious thing to do. If they believed that he really could read character in that way then it was clearly dangerous. If not, then it was equally clearly a waste of money. But, no doubt, they did it in much the same way that holiday-makers visit fortune-tellers at seaside resorts, as entertainment and without believing a word of it.

At any rate, it seems to have been a friendly occasion because, at the end of the session as Sinclair was following them to the door, Fowler offered him a drink. The offer was readily accepted and they had several. Afterwards, as the Professor left to resume his work, they agreed to meet again that evening.

Some hours later, as arranged, they met up again at the Ship and

Castle public-house. They had several more drinks together and during their conversation the two friendly strangers told Sinclair that they had just returned from abroad with a little money that they had made there. They were now looking for a suitable way to invest it. Since they were fond of moving around they were thinking in terms of some kind of travelling show. They had chosen their man well. All this was music to the ears of Sinclair who was always in need of money, especially as they had shown him handfuls of gold coins. He expressed the opinion that show-business would be an ideal investment but warned them to be careful, there were a lot of charlatans around.

In the circumstances it did not take them too long to reach an agreement to combine forces. It was even suggested that Fowler could be the 'strong man' of the show. A sort of 'Samson'.

Sinclair asked them where they were planning to sleep and, when told that they were looking for somewhere suitable to stay, invited them to 'Come along with me.' He took them to his own lodgings where he introduced them to his landlady, Mrs Lowell, as Scott and Taylor, two men supposedly having just returned from the Cape. They paid 10s a week in advance and Mrs Lowell had no trouble with them. They seemed to have pockets full of money, were never out late and were never drunk. Ideal lodgers. Fowler was obviously on his best behaviour following his mistake in Liverpool.

The Professor also introduced his new friends to Madame D'Arc and they began to assist him and his wife with their various acts, no doubt as 'members of the audience'. The Sinclairs were not, however, proving to be anywhere near the great attraction that they had claimed they would be. Madame D'Arc, having seen their act for herself, thought them second-rate and the rest of Cardiff seemed to agree with her. The vast crowds failed to make their appearance and Madame D'Arc sacked them after only two weeks of their four-week engagement.

This seemed to be the ideal moment for Milsom and Fowler to make their investment. It was agreed that, if Sinclair could find a suitable hall, they would split the cost and the eventual profits. So it was that, after only four days in Cardiff, Milsom and Fowler embarked once more on their travels.

On Tuesday, 10 March, Sinclair went on his own to Newport in search of a hall. In this he was successful and that same day was joined by the rest of the group, including a lady-friend of Fowler's. During the resulting show neither Milsom nor Fowler took part, but stood outside to drum up business.

The following Monday they travelled together to Pontypool but obviously things did not go according to plan because, later that same day, they moved to Bristol. At this point in their meanderings Fowler's lady-friend left them. The little group remained in Bristol a fortnight. Milsom took the opportunity on the first Sunday to go to see his wife and children in London. On the Monday, when he returned to Bristol, he brought his family back with him. On 30 March they moved again, this time to Swindon. Up until now the two burglars had been calling themselves Arthur Scott and Harry Taylor. Now they changed their names again, this time to Stevens and Mellish.

By now the two men were rapidly running out of money and this was causing growing friction with the Sinclairs. The shows that they were putting on were rarely profitable and Sinclair seemed to expect his companions to pay his rent as well as their own.

For her part Mrs Sinclair was somewhat less enamoured with her travelling companions than was her husband. But, as any criticism from her tended to bring immediate violence from him, she normally preferred to say nothing. Fowler also was sometimes violent. At Bristol, when he learned that Sinclair had no money and was looking to him to pay his debts, he chased him round the room and threatened him with a revolver, eventually firing it up the chimney.

While they were staying in Swindon, Milsom and Fowler tried and failed to break into a jeweller's shop. On 5 April, a Sunday, they went to Chippenham where, having no money, they spent the night in the station waiting-room. The next day they moved to Bath.

In the city of Bath they took rooms at 36 Monmouth Street, on the corner of St John's Place, leading down from the theatre. This was above a small confectionery and grocery shop kept by a Mrs Emma Warren. Albert Milsom, Emily and their two children, together with Mr and Mrs Sinclair, all shared one room. Fowler stayed elsewhere.

Although they did not know it, throughout their peregrinations round the country the police, in the form of P.C. Burrell, were never far behind. Their association with the Sinclairs, which had at first been an advantage since the police had been looking for two men on their own, was now a severe liability. A group of five adults and two children, travelling together and performing public entertainments at every town that they visit, is not inconspicuous.

As the police tracked them across the country, town by town, always just too late, it became increasingly obvious that it was only a matter of time. When the wanted men turned up at Bath on Easter

Monday their time was almost up. Over the next few days Milsom and Fowler hung around Stall Street, watching Mr Veal's jewellery shop at number 6a, noting the owner's movements and checking the back entrance, completely unaware that they themselves were being watched.

On Saturday, 10 April, Chief-Inspector Marshall of Scotland Yard, together with Inspector Nutkins of Kensal Town, travelled to Bath where they met up with P.C. Burrell. There was then a long consultation with senior local police officers. The following evening, as soon as it became dark, the police threw a tight cordon round number 36 and waited. Their men were instructed to allow anyone in, but no one out. At about eleven o'clock the watching police were delighted to see Fowler arrive and join his companions in the house. They were now all together – precisely what the police had been waiting for.

Taking absolutely no chances, the police were there in force. Six officers, Chief-Inspector Marshall, Chief-Inspector Noble, Detective-Inspector Mountfield, Inspector Newport, Inspector Nutkins and P.C. Burrell were to carry out the raid. It was an extraordinary collection of senior officers which must have made P.C. Burrell feel the odd man out, but he had certainly earned the right to be in 'at the kill'. It is difficult to believe that a similar 'raiding-force' could occur today.

The six men, all carrying loaded revolvers, burst their way through the door. They rushed up the stairs, Nutkins in the lead and crashed into the room at the top. They achieved complete surprise. The occupants of the room were standing, talking together in front of the fire. Each officer had a specific target and made for him. Inspector Newport rushed for Fowler, known to be the most dangerous. As he seized him, Fowler resisted and reached for a revolver lying on the mantelpiece. Chief-Inspector Marshall, coming up behind, smashed the butt of his revolver on Fowler's head and he dropped, crashing to the floor.

Nutkins, meanwhile, had grabbed Milsom and pointed his gun at the man's head. Milsom gave no more trouble. None of the others put up any resistance, although the children screamed at the top of their voices.

All were arrested. Fowler, apparently still unconscious and bleeding profusely from his head wound, was taken to the Royal United Hospital under a heavy police guard. The rest went to the local police station to be joined within a few hours by the now heavily bandaged, but not badly injured, Fowler.

In the room above the Monmouth Street shop was found a black Gladstone bag. It contained a stock and bit, chisel, jemmy, gimlet and a knife evidently used for forcing window-catches. A complete burglar's kit.

Their recorded personal possessions were, in the case of Albert Milsom, a knife, $3\frac{1}{2}$d in coin, a belt, four collars, one umbrella, a handkerchief and two metal rings. Fowler's treasures comprised a six-chambered revolver with 100 bullets, a broken stick, a brass pin and an umbrella.

Professor Sinclair and his wife were both released early on Monday afternoon. It was quite obvious that neither of them had any idea of the real identity or character of the two men with whom they had been travelling for the last month or so.

Milsom and Fowler were both charged with murder, Emily Milsom with being an accessory after the fact. Upon being charged, Fowler declared:

'I do not know anything about it. I was not with Milsom. I was at a lodging-house in Kensal Town and am innocent of the charge.'

Chief-Inspector Marshall told him:

'Give me the address where you lodged or stayed that night. I will take care to fetch any witnesses that there may be on your behalf.'

To this offer Fowler could only answer:

'I don't know the name of the lodging-house or of the people who keep it.'

When the time came to convey the prisoners to London, large crowds flocked to see them. First at Bath, when they were taken to the railway station and placed in a sealed compartment with a large police escort. Then, upon their arrival at Paddington where, having been given notice of their arrival, the crowd was even larger. And, finally, when they reached Highgate Police Station where they were formally charged.

About a fortnight later, after appearances in the magistrates' court at Highgate which had made it quite clear just how much evidence the police had accumulated, Milsom wrote to Chief-Inspector Marshall offering to confess. On 28 April Marshall accordingly went to Holloway Prison where Milsom was being held and, in company with Inspector Nutkins, heard a full and lengthy confession. Besides other information Milsom told them how he and Fowler had buried their tools in the shrubbery and gave precise directions as to where they could be found. It did not take the police too long to find them. Amongst other items, they comprised two chisels and two bradawls. The larger of the two chisels still had blood-stains on it.

Fowler's response, when he heard of Milsom's confession, was to remark bitterly to a police-escort:

My pal, the dirty dog, has turned Queen's evidence and our mouthpiece is no use. But I can tell a tale as well as he. There was £112 in the bag in the safe and I gave him £53 and some shillings which was an equal share of the money after what I had spent. Is it likely that I should give that to a man who stood outside? He put his foot on the old man's neck until he made sure he was dead and then we went upstairs, he first, and found the old man's trousers with the keys of the safe in the pocket. But thieves will cut one another's throats for half a loaf.

Shortly afterwards, left alone in his cell, Fowler removed his neck-tie and endeavoured to hang himself with it. It was only with considerable difficulty that the warders were able to prevent him.

Emily Milsom was discharged before the trial, possibly in return for her husband's confession. He claimed all along that she had known nothing of his involvement in the Muswell Hill crime. There was, in any case, virtually no evidence against her. It is true that she did 'dispose of' Fowler's blood-stained clothing, but had she known its recent history it was presumed she would not have pawned it and deposited the ticket in a teapot for anyone to find. But it is nevertheless to Milsom's credit that he did at all times exhibit concern for his family's welfare, even if his human concern never extended to anyone else.

The trial, when it came at the Old Bailey on 19 May, took an entirely predictable course. The prosecution had successfully constructed an overwhelming case, with a mass of evidence, against which the defence could not reasonably hope to make much impression. When, at last, the jury retired to consider its verdict Milsom was seen to say something to a warder and smile. Fowler also saw the incident and reacted with total fury. He made a desperate attempt to get at his former accomplice. His ferocious struggles were so great that his warders were unable to contain him and had to be augmented by several policemen.

The verdict of the jury was an inevitable 'Guilty'. Both men were sentenced to death and were hanged together, side by side, on 10 June.

What is there to be said about Milsom and Fowler? They were typical of what the Victorians called the criminal classes. Their most obvious characteristics were a total lack of conscience coupled with gross stupidity. Given that they were so well known to the police and, in the case of Fowler, still on parole, even committing the burglary showed a complete lack of common-sense. Their fondness for leaving evidence lying around waiting to be found, and ostentatiously spending large sums of gold immediately after the crime, made detection inevitable.

Should Milsom have been hanged? There is certainly no reason for believing that he played any active part in the murder of Henry Smith. Violence was not at all his style. He was essentially a weak man who allowed himself to be dominated by his companion.

At the same time, he knew perfectly well when he set out that night what kind of man Fowler was. He must have known that, should they be disturbed by a member of the household, Fowler would not have the sense to run away. Fowler had, after all, only just emerged from Dartmoor after serving a sentence for burglary with violence.

Even in his lengthy confession, the basis for much of the above account, Milsom expresses not one word of regret for the brutal fate of Henry Smith. While the murder was being committed he did nothing whatever to try to stop it. Afterwards when, according to his own account, he returned to the house and found Fowler covered in blood the idea of attempting to save Henry Smith from dying never entered his head. He was interested only in getting his share of the spoils. Murder meant no more to him than it did to Fowler. He just lacked the courage to do it himself.

Throughout his long and detailed confession Milsom tried to portray Fowler as the only real villain. He, himself, was just someone who, against his better judgement, allowed himself to be talked into taking part. Given his long criminal record this is not easily believable. At the trial several residents of Tetherdown claimed to have seen both Fowler and Milsom acting suspiciously in the area several days before the crime occurred. This is certainly easier to believe than Milsom's story that he knew nothing of the planned burglary until the evening that it took place.

The attempt to escape justice by running away was doomed to failure. Its first effect was to draw attention to themselves. Men do not run away for nothing. Had they succeeded in getting abroad, perhaps to Australia or South Africa, they might have stood a chance. It is difficult, however, to believe that Milsom would desert his wife and family for long. But the days when two wanted men could commit a murder and then hide elsewhere in the country were long gone. Modern communications and increasing co-operation between different police authorities were rapidly turning England into a very small country indeed for a wanted man. During their wanderings with Professor Sinclair they were living on borrowed time. At Bath their time finally ran out.

THE WARSAW RESTAURANT

THE WARSAW RESTAURANT

t around eight o'clock on the morning of New Year's Day 1911, Police-Constable Joseph Mumford began the part of his beat which led him across London's Clapham Common. It was a very lonely walk. At that time of the year it is barely light at eight o'clock and not only was it New Year's Day, many people having a 'lie-in' following the previous night's revelry, it was also a Sunday.

By ten past eight he was walking amongst the dark, leafless trees surrounding the band-stand which, looking rather incongruous in the cold winter light, only served to increase the loneliness. Leaving the band-stand behind him, he started along the path leading towards the north-west corner of the common and Battersea Rise. The path, which was asphalted, was separated from the cricket-pitch on his right by a low railing. To his left lay a part of the common that was still wild, with small trees and large clumps of gorse amongst the long, wet grass.

He had not progressed far along the path when he saw the figure of a man lying between the gorse bushes about twelve feet from the path. P.C. Mumford went to have a closer look, thinking that a tramp or drunk ought to have been able to find somewhere better to sleep on a cold winter's night.

But even before he reached the recumbent figure he knew that he had a dead man on his hands and a closer look quickly confirmed his first impression. The man lay on his back, his head a hideous mess of massive wounds caked with blood. Purely as a matter of form, the policeman knelt down, picked up the man's arm at the wrist and felt for a pulse. He had quite clearly been dead for some time.

Returning to the still deserted footpath, P.C. Mumford discovered a large patch of blood near the railings which were, themselves, unstained. There were two distinct parallel tracks etched into the turf, clearly showing that the body had been dragged from the path across to the bushes. Once more the policeman returned to the body. It was of a man in his fifties, with grey hair, a dark moustache and a dark foreign-looking complexion.

A large black handkerchief with red stripes lay folded across the top of his head and was tucked tightly under the collar of his coat, partly covering the side of his face. The collar of the heavy overcoat was turned up and reached almost to the top of the man's head, as though it had been used to drag the body to its present position.

The man's right hand lay twisted beneath him, his left resting by his side. His legs were crossed at the ankles. The overcoat had a great deal of blood on it, while the knees of his trousers were thick with mud. The toes of his boots, which had been shiny, were caked in mud. Lying amongst the bushes, about ten feet from the body, was a bowler hat. Satisfied that he had seen all that could be seen without moving the body, Mumford made for the nearest telephone and called for assistance.

The preliminary examination on the common revealed that not only had the victim been severely beaten about the head he had also been repeatedly stabbed; the corpse was then removed to the mortuary for a more thorough investigation. The police surgeon who arrived on the scene at nine o'clock expressed the opinion that the man had most probably been dead for six hours.

While the police awaited the result of the post-mortem and any further information that that might bring them, they made a careful examination of the man's clothing, looking for some clue as to his possible identity. The clothing comprised a black Melton overcoat with an astrakhan collar, a dark striped jacket and waistcoat, dark muffler, blue trousers and patent leather boots. There was also the bowler hat which bore the name of an Upton Park tailor and a pipe, also found close to the body, which he had apparently been smoking and which, like much else, was blood-stained.

The contents of his pockets were not of much immediate assistance to them. There was a notebook which appeared to record small financial transactions but which carried no clue to the identity of its owner. In one of his pockets were the remnants of a ham sandwich and in one of the jacket pockets they discovered a crumpled-up scrap of paper with a few words scrawled in pencil upon it. The words were barely legible but seemed to include 'boots' and 'coke'.

What the police did not find (and this seemed likely to be significant) was money, apart that is from one solitary half-penny. Also conspicuous by its absence was a watch and chain. At the beginning of the century any man would have felt half-naked without his watch and chain; it was a symbol both of masculinity and of respectability. Even if a man could not afford a watch he still had his chain which crossed his manly chest in a suitably impressive manner and disappeared into his left breast-pocket. Providing that nobody asked him the time he kept his self-esteem and, of course, the very act of having to ask the time was, itself, an admission of not owning a watch and chain and therefore of having an inferior status. Judging by his clothes the victim, while obviously somewhat poor, was by no means poverty stricken – he should have sported a watch and chain. The motive for the murder was therefore most likely to have been theft. Or was it?

Everything about the body, from the foreign complexion, the name and address of the hatter, the choice of clothing and the man's whole appearance, clearly indicated that he was Jewish. In 1911 that meant that he most likely lived in the Stepney or Whitechapel area, very much a Jewish enclave. And to the police in the winter of 1910–11 the word Stepney meant anarchists and the Houndsditch murders.

Every age has its own peculiar brand of political extremists, our own age by no means excepted. Around the turn of the century, and indeed for some time previously, one such group of revolutionaries termed themselves anarchists. They claimed to be opposed to all kinds of political authority and frequently exhibited their beliefs by indulging in assassination and terrorism. Like most political extremists of their day, they were at their strongest in Russia and Eastern Europe, appearing in Western Europe largely in the form of refugees or fugitives from justice, or what passed for justice in the countries where they originated.

Such men and women were by no means uncommon in cities like Paris and London where they were not actively pursued by the authorities. The English viewed anarchism in the same way as they habitually regard anything ending in 'ism', with slightly amused indifference. An occupation for harmless, eccentric foreigners who do not have the good fortune to understand more important activities like cricket or football.

During the evening of 6 December 1910, P.C. Walter Piper was on duty in Bishopsgate when he was approached by a Mr Max Weil who carried on a fancy goods business from a warehouse in Exchange Buildings, a cul-de-sac behind Houndsditch. Mr Weil reported strange banging and scraping noises from a next-door premises, premises which should rightly be empty. The building concerned backed on to a large jeweller's shop in Houndsditch and the possible implications were obvious.

P.C. Piper went with Mr Weil to investigate. With the normal caution of policemen he first visited Mr Weil's own premises and heard the strange noises for himself. Satisfied on that point he then turned his attention to the adjoining building. Approaching the dark and apparently empty house he knocked on the door. After some delay it was opened a few inches. P.C. Piper asked, 'Is the missus in?'. The reply in broken English was, 'She's gone out.' 'Right, I'll call back later,' said the policeman.

Within a short time the police had the building completely surrounded and prepared themselves to arrest a gang of burglars. 'Leave it in our hands, we will see to it,' Sergeant Bentley told Mr Weil. But the police were not dealing with a group of English burglars who played to English rules and would readily give up when faced by a police cordon. Instead, when the unarmed policemen attempted to enter the premises they were greeted by bursts of fire from automatic weapons which left them three dead and another two badly wounded. In the process the anarchists, who had been intending to finance their political activities by a jewel robbery, escaped.

Over the following days a massive police hunt swept the area. One of the leaders of the gang was found dead, having been accidentally hit by a stray bullet from a colleague's gun, and gradually other members were tracked down and apprehended. The principal members of the group, including the colourfully named Peter the Painter, remained, however, very much at large. It followed that any unusual event involving a foreigner immediately raised the question of its possible connection with the Houndsditch killers.

During the afternoon of New Year's Day, only a few hours after the discovery of the crime, three police officers from Clapham journeyed north of the river to consult with their opposite numbers at Leman Street Police Station in Whitechapel. They were Inspector Ward, Sergeant Cooper and Sergeant Hawkins. Here they met up with Inspector Leeson and Sergeant Boreham. Leeson, together with a long-term colleague, Detective-Inspector Wensley, was already heavily involved in the hunt for the remaining anarchists. While originating in Putney, an area in west London that could hardly be more different from his present beat, he had been stationed in Whitechapel since he had joined the force.

The burly inspector who had, over the years, become something of an expert on the Jewish community, was very well known and much respected by the local people. He had even acquired a smattering of Yiddish, an immense advantage when working in a community whose English was often severely limited.

As a result of the conference the two groups of officers agreed their initial strategy. Inspector Ward and his colleagues in Brixton would concentrate on trying to trace any possible witnesses to the crime, while Inspector Leeson would endeavour to identify the murdered man.

On the face of it, he did not have very much to go on except, that is, for that crumpled, grubby scrap of paper. 'Boots', 'Coke'. What could it mean? A rudimentary shopping list? Leeson had an idea. Grabbing his hat and taking Sergeant Boreham with him, he strode quickly up Leman Street, crossed the road, took a short cut through a series of side streets and found himself in Commercial Road. Threading their way through the tangle of carts and horse-buses they crossed the road, slipped through a narrow alley and emerged in a short street of some twelve decrepit houses. On the wall of one of the dirty little buildings could be seen a faded sign, Coke Street.

So far, so good. They looked along the two rows of dingy buildings and saw just what they were looking for, a boot and shoe repairer. Entering the dark little shop, they were soon greeted by the proprietor as he emerged from an even darker room beyond. An old man who, it soon became apparent, spoke not a word of English. Leeson, putting his long studies to good use, began to question him in Yiddish.

'Know anything about that?' he asked, handing over the grubby piece of paper.

The man peered at it, with weak eyes.

'Yes,' he said, 'I gave this paper to a customer of mine as a receipt for a pair of boots. I've still got the boots. He hasn't called for them yet. They are ready. Do you want them?'

'No thanks,' said Leeson. 'What I want is the name and address of the man who left them.'

The old man shrugged his shoulders. 'They just left the boots and were to call back for them when ready.'

'But don't you remember the man? Didn't he give you his name at all? Please try and think. It is most important.'

'I can't be sure. I think he told me his name. It was something like Peron or Deron. I think it was Beron. Yes, that's what it was, Beron, and I think he mentioned that he lived in Black Lion Yard.'

The two police officers left the shop and paused outside, feeling rather pleased with themselves. It was proving much easier than they had expected. Black Lion Yard. Oh, yes, they knew that all right. Every policeman in the district knew Black Lion Yard. It was a narrow street off the Whitechapel Road, with about a dozen houses in it, every one of them occupied by a receiver of stolen goods. The police spent a lot of their time going in and out of Black Lion Yard and much good it did them.

But when they went there, it proved to be even more of a waste of time than such visits usually were. They were told that Beron had moved, to where no one knew. Even not very gentle hints about police searches failed to produce any further information. He had simply moved.

So, back to normal police work. The hard grind. Visit all the shops in the area, there seemed to be hundreds. All the grubby little cafés. And question, question, question. It was desperately boring, it was hard on the feet, but it worked.

It was in a greengrocer's shop in Sidney Street that Leeson learned about the Beron brothers. There were, he was told, three of them: Leon, Solomon and David. They lived together above another greengrocer's in nearby Jubilee Street, but when the police visited, they were out. Enquiries in the tiny shop below revealed that they were usually out all day and did not normally return before midnight.

Late that evening, Leeson and Sergeant Boreham once more made their way to Jubilee Street and let themselves into the premises with a key provided by the landlord. The place was deserted, very scruffy and rather dirty. They settled themselves down as best as they could for a long wait. Time passed slowly, ten o'clock, eleven o'clock, midnight. From time to time they heard footsteps in the road outside, but always they passed by. One o'clock, still nothing. Two o'clock. Were they wasting their time, wouldn't they be better off in bed? Wait. Listen.

Footsteps outside, approaching the building; a key in the lock, the door opening. Two men, even darker shapes against the dark. Two police torches pierce the gloom. Two startled men, justifiably afraid, not knowing what they had walked into and only slightly calmed at being told that it was the police. Then questions, identities.

They are Solomon and David Beron. Yes, they do have a brother, Leon, but don't know where he is. Inspector Leeson told the two brothers that a man had been murdered on Clapham Common and that he had reason to believe that the man might well be the missing Leon. Then, deciding that he had already spent more than enough time in the discomfort of Jubilee Street, he took them to the relative luxury of his office in Leman Street. Once in the warmth of the police station both brothers became more relaxed, even friendly. They were completely co-operative and quite clearly wished to help.

They soon confirmed what little the police already knew about them and were able to give a fairly detailed account of their brother's life. Their family was indeed Jewish, originating in Russia. Not long after Leon's birth in 1863 their parents, tiring of the constant anti-semitism, left Russia and settled in Paris where the family continued to live for the next thirty years. In 1894 they moved across the channel, ostensibly in pursuit of a legendary claim to an estate worth £26,000 and settled in London. Their mother was now dead and their father had been placed in a Jewish home for the infirm three years before. In addition to the three brothers, there were also two sisters, one of them married.

Leon was a widower, his wife having died some years before. He spoke very little English and no Russian, but was fluent in French as well as his native Yiddish. According to his brother Solomon, his income came from the rents on nine houses in Russell Grove. He had bought these in 1897 and they brought him in the vast sum of 6s or 7s a week. He normally collected his rents on Saturday evenings and, having no bank account, always carried his money with him. At the time of his death, Solomon thought, his brother would probably have about £12 in gold on him. He also wore a gold watch which had an 1887 £5 gold piece fastened to the chain. Altogether, this would be worth £30 or £40.

The most obvious explanation for the murder was that Beron had taken a short cut through the common. There, he had been waylaid and murdered by a casual criminal intent upon robbery. But what was he doing there? No one who knew him could think of any reason why he should go to Clapham in the day-time, let alone in the middle of the night.

The path where the crime took place was a very popular spot in the summer. Men playing or watching cricket, women exercising dogs, nurses in uniform pushing prams or supervising small children romping on the grass. In the winter months local people simply used it as a short cut. But after dark it was shunned. Lonely and completely unlit, with trees close to the path, it would be foolish to risk such a route, especially when a well-lit road was readily available.

Had someone deliberately lured him to the lonely spot with the specific intention of murdering him? If that were the case, then it must be someone he knew and trusted. His two brothers were soon eliminated from the list of possible suspects; they both had excellent alibis, David in particular. He had been attending a wedding celebration in Stepney which lasted until four in the morning. Dozens of people saw him there.

During their journey from Jubilee Street to the police station Solomon told the inspector of a little café in Osborn Street where his brother spent a great deal of time. The Warsaw Restaurant. It was to that very modest establishment that Inspector Leeson next directed his attention.

The Whitechapel and Spitalfields districts of east London have for many centuries provided an enclave for newly arrived immigrants; for people who, for some reason or another, usually political or religious persecution, choose to move to this island on the edge of Europe. Here they believe that they have a chance of living, working and bringing up their families in peace and freedom. For the newcomers the area is a bridgehead in a strange land. Their children, growing-up in England with a command of the English language far superior to that of their parents, tend to leave the area and become, to a greater or lesser extent, merged with the general population of cosmopolitan London.

In the fifteenth and sixteenth centuries the refugees were Flemings and Huguenots. Today, although greatly changed by bombing and redevelopment, the East End has a large Asian population. At the beginning of the century it was inhabited to a great extent by Jews, principally of East European origin, tired of the endless pogroms of Poland and Russia. Each of these successive waves of poor immigrants has relied on the same industry to sustain them. The clothing industry. It requires little capital to set up and only a steady stream of young women, prepared to work long hours and ruin their eyesight for a pittance, to maintain it.

Osborn Street was in the centre of this Jewish enclave, the Warsaw Restaurant one of many which served the population. It was not one of those English restaurants in which you are expected to eat your meal quickly and leave immediately, the proprietor hovering over you disapprovingly if you linger over your coffee. The Warsaw Restaurant was an East European café – groups of men stayed for hours, sometimes all day, with just an occasional cup of tea or bowl of soup to help keep the proprietor solvent. As the owner of the café was later to explain in court, 'I cannot turn a man out just because he hasn't any money.'

The men did business there, sometimes just within the law, sometimes outside it. But mostly they talked about the places and people that they had left behind – Warsaw, St Petersburg, Prague and Vienna. They also talked and argued about politics. Not the English kind. There was no discussion here about the respective merits of Liberalism or Conservatism, no free trade, no budget or the problem of Ireland. It was raw politics. Here men were Socialists, Anarchists, Communists. They talked of revolutions and the end of dynasties. Talking in a wide range of languages, French, German, Polish, Russian, but mainly Yiddish, they had little fear of being overheard. Any stranger would be highly conspicuous and, in any case, the British authorities were not much interested.

But it was, for the most part, just talk. Like the rest of the population of England, their real concern was for their families. How to keep their wives happy and how to bring up their children. Even at the nearby self-proclaimed Anarchist Club, in which some of the Houndsditch killers had been in the habit of meeting and which was forcibly closed by the authorities, the activities were remarkably harmless. They drank tea or lemonade, staged left-wing plays and held a dance once a week.

After his long talk with the Beron brothers, Leeson retired to his home for a badly needed sleep and then, suitably refreshed, set out for the Warsaw Restaurant in search of information. At first glance it was hardly imposing, the usual run-down, elderly two-storey building, badly in need of a coat of paint. Entering, he found himself at the bar where cakes, bread and butter and similar light snacks were sold. Also tea, coffee or lemonade. No alcohol was available and enquiries revealed that while some could always be sent out for if requested, it very rarely was. Beyond the bar there were fourteen or fifteen tables, each with its quota of chairs, no two of which seemed to match.

A number of customers were sitting around and gazed with evident interest at the new arrival. They soon proved to be both friendly and helpful. The restaurant was run by a Russian, Alex Snelwar, whom Leeson already knew quite well. He told the inspector that Leon Beron had been a regular customer there for some years. He had all his meals there. It was his habit to arrive at the café at about two o'clock in the afternoon and stay there until midnight. He had been doing this for the last six years. Occasionally he would go out for half an hour but, for the rest of the time, he just sat and talked to the other customers.

Although he spent very little money, only about 1s-6d a day at the restaurant and 2s-9d a week in rent, he had the reputation of being well-off. He did nothing to discourage this strange belief. His money was kept in a leather purse which was fastened to his waistcoat by a safety-pin and the other customers had often seen the large number of gold coins it contained, £40 or £50, Snelwar thought. Everyone was also very familiar with his large gold watch and chain, complete with its £5 piece. In the restaurant he was always called 'the landlord'.

Inspector Leeson asked if Beron had any particular friends. One of the few women customers remarked:

'The last time I saw him, the night before last I think it was, he was with a tall man who wore a coat like yours, except his had a belt and yours hasn't.'

'I know the man you mean,' said another customer. 'It's the Australian.'

To Leeson this was getting more and more interesting. He knew the 'Australian' all right. Six months' hard labour for burglary in the name of Morris Tagger, five years for attempted burglary in the name of Morris Stein. Real name believed to be Alexander Petropavlov. He had not been out long, only released on parole on 17 September. Just to be sure that they were talking about the same man, he asked a few more questions. Do they know his name? What does he look like?

'Steinie Morrison,' they said. Very tall, 6' 3'', dark, clean-shaven, rather good-looking young man. They first began seeing him in November and he soon became a regular. Seemed to be cultivating a friendship with Leon Beron who was normally rather 'a loner'. He took to calling in two or three times a day to take his meals there, always sharing a table with the murdered man. Only a few days before the murder he had been observed examining with great interest the £5 coin attached to Beron's watch–chain.

Morris Stein, Steinie Morrison, and the description fitted perfectly. Leeson returned to his office feeling pleased with his efforts, certain that he was on the track of Beron's murderer. The next day, however, Leeson was off the case. He was off all his cases. The

Houndsditch anarchists had been found, with dramatic consequences.

The search for Peter the Painter and his associates had been progressing steadily. On 27 December, at a house in Gold Street, Stepney, a 'bomb factory' had been found. On 30 December three men and two women made their first appearance in court at Guildhall. And finally, on 2 January while Leeson had been busy with the Beron case, his colleagues at Leman Street received a 'tip-off'. The anarchists were at a house in Sidney Street, only yards from the greengrocer's shop where Leeson had first learned about the Beron brothers.

Early the next morning the police spread a tight cordon around the area and quietly evacuated the adjoining houses. The ground floor of the target house was successfully emptied, 100 policemen guarded every exit, though engaged more with the task of keeping sightseers out than anarchists in. At 7.30 a.m. the police, led by Inspector Leeson and his friend Detective-Inspector Wensley, prepared to make their arrests.

Unfortunately, as in Houndsditch, they failed to understand the kind of men they were dealing with. They calmly walked up to the house and hammered on the door. There was no reply. Perhaps, they thought, the criminals are still asleep. Picking up handfuls of gravel, they proceeded to throw them at the bedroom windows. It was a mistake, the wanted men were not asleep. The rattle of gravel was answered by a hail of bullets from automatic pistols and Inspector Leeson fell, shot in the lung and foot. As his colleagues struggled, amidst continuing gunfire from the house, to drag him to safety, Leeson turned to Detective-Inspector Wensley who had been his friend since they had been constables together on the beat. 'I am dying. Goodbye, give my love to the children. Bury me at Putney.'

Luckily he was wrong. He did not die, he lived to write his memoirs which helped to produce this account, but his police career was over.

The anarchists were eventually dealt with after a seven-hour siege, but not before the intervention of the Scots Guards and the Home Secretary, a certain Winston Churchill, who demonstrated his fondness for being at the centre of the action. The house caught fire, two bodies were found in the ashes, but Peter the Painter, if he ever existed, was conspicuous by his absence.

With Inspector Leeson out of action, the Beron case was taken over by his long-term friend, Detective-Inspector Wensley, a tall slim man who was destined to become one of the most famous of Scotland Yard detectives and, in due course, Chief Constable of that renowned establishment.

By now the police had received the post-mortem report which did not provide pleasant reading. It showed that the unfortunate man had received no less than eight blows, of considerable violence, on the head, probably from a jemmy or small crowbar. These had inflicted terrible damage, the whole of the left side of the face had been battered in and the left ear was almost completely severed. He had also received a violent blow on the mouth that had smashed his teeth. Not content, his assailant had then stabbed the already dead man three times in the heart and twice in the right-hand side of the chest. Marks forming a rough 'S' shape had been cut into his cheeks.

The presence of a quantity of mud on the dead man's coat and the tips of his boots, together with clear marks on the ground, indicated that he had been attacked while walking along the path. Having been killed, he was then dragged by the arms, face down, into the bushes, before being turned over onto his back and robbed. The stomach contained partly digested food, probably bread or cake, and a considerable amount of alcohol. Death had occurred at about 3.00 a.m.

The 'S' marks on the dead man's face were to provide a subject for endless speculation, both at the time and since. There were those, anxious to link the murder to the anarchists, who attached great importance to them, pointing out that the word 'spy' begins with the letter 'S', not only in English but also in many other languages, including Russian and Yiddish. The anarchists, like most subversives, were obsessed with the possible presence of traitors in their midst and could never believe that their operation in Houndsditch was foiled by an alert neighbour and an intelligent police constable. They had to have been betrayed.

According to the theory, they blamed Beron who had been acting as a receiver for them, had him lured to the common and murdered him, carving the letter 'S' as a warning to others. On the other hand, people with a less colourful imagination, including the police, attached little importance to the marks, pointing out that the 'S' was far from clear and that such a shape could have arisen simply by the knife hitting the cheekbone.

The search for the killer soon led Wensley to the Warsaw Restaurant where the proprietor, Alex Snelwar, his waiters and customers proved to be extremely helpful. Much more so than could have been reasonably expected. They were, after all, members of a close-knit group, separated by nationality and religion from the majority of the population of London. Their experiences with the police in the countries from which they came must have made them suspicious about the methods and motives of the law-enforcement officers. And yet, thanks to their help, within a very short time D.I. Wensley had not only a very definite suspect but a great deal of extremely valuable evidence.

On the day of Beron's death, Morrison had been in and out of the café all day. He came in once more at 6.30 p.m., this time carrying a parcel. This he gave to a waiter, Joseph Mintz, saying, 'Give me that back when I go away.' The proprietor's ten-year-old daughter, Becky, with the natural curiosity of children, asked what was in it. 'A flute,' he told her. Joseph Mintz knew perfectly well that, whatever was in the parcel, it was certainly not a flute. The parcel was 2 feet long, 4 or 5 inches in circumference and was wrapped in brown paper. It was surprisingly heavy, as heavy as an iron bar.

Morrison immediately walked across to the table where Beron was seated and remained there, talking to him the rest of the evening. Between eight and nine he called for two glasses of tea with lemon and, at about 11.40 p.m., for a glass of lemonade. At approximately a quarter to twelve the two men were seen by several people in the restaurant to get up and leave the premises together. Before departing Morrison collected his brown-paper parcel from the waiter.

An hour later a butcher, Jacob Weisberg, was strolling with a friend in Whitechapel Road when they saw Morrison and Beron walking together in a westerly direction. Nothing was then seen of either man until, at about 1.30 a.m., Samuel Rosen, a cabinet-maker who had earlier seen the two men together in the restaurant, saw them again, this time in Brick Lane, Spitalfields. They were walking towards the Whitechapel Road.

Not long after, they were seen again. Samuel and Nellie Deitch had been to a New Year's Eve party in Commercial Road. They left the party at 1.30 and set off home together along Commercial Road in the direction of Whitechapel Road. At the corner of Philpot Street Mrs Deitch remarked to her husband, 'That's Mr Beron with a friend.' She had made this comment because she was used to seeing Beron on his own. The two men must have heard her remark because the other, much taller man, turned and looked at her.

At a quarter to two, a waiter from the Warsaw Restaurant,

sixteen-year-old Jack Taw, was standing at a coffee-stall in White-chapel Road at the corner of Church Lane. He observed Beron and Morrison on the other side of the road, walking towards Mile End.

The police now knew that, at 1.45 a.m., Beron was walking with Morrison in the Whitechapel Road. By three o'clock he was lying dead on Clapham Common. Somehow, during that missing hour and a quarter, he must have travelled that not inconsiderable distance, five or six miles. Clearly he could not have walked it, he must have used some means of transport. At two o'clock in the morning that could only have been a cab.

It was in this aspect of the case that D.I. Ward showed his worth. He had pamphlets produced offering a reward of £1 for information; these were distributed amongst the cab-drivers in their favourite haunts. Reports soon began to come in, some worthless, some irrelevent, but some very helpful.

Shortly after two o'clock on the morning of New Year's Day Edward Hayman was driving his hansom-cab along Mile End Road. He had come to the East End with a passenger and, having dropped him, was on the look-out for further business, preferably something that would take him back to his normal hunting-ground south of the river. Near the junction of Mile End Road and Sidney Street he saw another cab stop for a moment near two men standing on the pavement. The taller of the two men seemed to speak to the cab-driver for a moment, but the cab drove off without them.

Mr Hayman turned his own vehicle round, drove back to where the men were still standing and asked if they required a cab. The taller of the two men, who answered the description of Morrison, said, 'I will give you 5s to drive to Lavender Hill.' As this was precisely the area that Mr Hayman was planning to go to anyway, he wasted little time in agreeing. The two men then climbed into the cab and they set off through the City, across London Bridge and on through south London to Lavender Hill. At the corner of Lavender Gardens the tall man asked him to stop. The men then alighted from the cab, the driver received his 5s and drove off. It was now a quarter to three.

Lavender Gardens is almost opposite the north-west corner of Clapham Common and the path leading to the band-stand. The path where, at about three o'clock, Leon Beron met a violent death.

Early that same morning, Alfred Stephens sat in his cab at Clapham Cross, the other side of the common from Lavender Gardens. At about twenty past three he saw a man walking from the direction of the common. He enquired of the man whether he wanted a cab. The man did not answer but, after walking on a little way, turned around, walked back and climbed into the cab. The driver was told to take him to Kennington. This was straight down the Clapham Road towards the centre of London, a distance of about two miles. The tall passenger left the cab between the Hanover Arms and the Oval tube-station. After paying the 2s fare, the man walked behind the cab and set off in the direction of Kennington Church and Camberwell Road.

But he did not seem to have walked far. Only a few minutes later, now in the company of another man, he approached the cab-rank near Kennington Church and asked a driver how much it would cost to drive to Finsbury Park Station, on the other side of London. Seven shillings he was told. He seemed to hesitate, obviously thinking that it was a lot of money, but his companion had no such doubts. He almost pushed the tall man into the cab and then joined him himself. The two passengers were eventually dropped in the Seven Sisters Road where the driver was paid his fare in the form of three half-crowns.

It was a curious fact that, while prior to the murder Morrison had been in the habit of taking all his meals in the Warsaw Restaurant and spending many hours there, from that moment on he never again dined there. Only once was he ever seen there again. That was at ten o'clock on the morning after the murder when he stepped in for a moment, looked around and then immediately left, without saying a word to anyone.

The police did not find it at all surprising that Morrison left his lodgings immediately after the crime and apparently told no one where he was going. But he did not, in fact, go very far. On 6 January the police learned that he had deposited some clothing at a laundry in the East End. It was run by a Russian named Max Mannis and was called, for some inexplicable reason, 'The Japanese Laundry'. Morrison had given an address in Newark Street.

A careful watch was therefore kept on 91 Newark Street which was occupied by Mr and Mrs Zimmerman. It was a longish wait but two days later, on the morning of 8 January, the watching officers saw Morrison leave the house. They followed him at a discreet distance. He made first for the Japanese laundry where he collected the clothing that he had left there, then, with the police still at his heels, he went to a restaurant in Fieldgate Street and ordered breakfast. It was now nine o'clock.

Morrison was by no means a stranger there. The proprietors, Mr and Mrs Cohen, had at one time been used to him dining there every day. At the beginning of November, however, he had suddenly stopped coming and they did not see him again until the New Year. Then he once more appeared but for only one meal. During the course of conversation he told Mrs Cohen that he was an actor and singer and had been performing in Italy. He then once more vanished and was not seen again until his sudden arrival on the 8th. As he sat eating his leisurely breakfast, he had a Gladstone bag and a brown-paper parcel by his side.

Finishing his meal, he leaned back in his seat with an air of quiet satisfaction and placed his hands in his trouser pockets. A moment later five armed police officers stormed into the little café and seized him. Surprise was complete. One moment he was relaxing after a pleasant breakfast, the next he was sitting handcuffed and sur-rounded by police. He kept saying, 'Don't put anything in my pockets.' He was then conveyed to Leman Street Police Station where he was informed that he would be detained while they awaited the arrival of D.I. Ward from Brixton.

While waiting, he asked to see D.I. Wensley and made a statement. In it he claimed to be an Australian citizen, having been born in Sydney. He said that during the autumn of 1910 he had worked as a baker's roundsman and left of his own accord when he had saved £4. This large capital sum he had used to begin trading in cheap jewellery. He had lived at 91 Newark Street until 1 January when he began living with a girl named Florrie at 116 York Road, Lambeth. The night before his arrest he stayed with a friend, Mrs Cinnamon of Grove Street, because it had been too late to return to his lodgings.

The trade in cheap jewellery was Morrison's explanation for the fact that, while in December he had obviously been short of money, he pawned a gold chain on 23 December and was suddenly prosperous in the New Year. Early in January, Morrison cashed a cheque for a second-hand clothes' dealer, Isaac Flitterman, paying him with eight half-sovereigns. He had at first offered him a £5 note but Mr Flitterman had never seen one before and did not know what it was.

When informed that he was to be charged with the murder of Leon Beron and asked to hand over his clothes for examination, he asked:

'What do you want to take them from me for?'

'There are spots of blood on the cuff, also on your collar and tie.'

'That's not blood at all. That is mud that I got yesterday.'

The next day an identity parade was held, during the course of which no less than ten potential witnesses correctly identified Morrison. Eight of them, including the three cab-drivers and Mr and Mrs Deitch, were prepared to swear that they saw him in the company of the murdered man on the night of his death. It was only learned much later that the three cab-drivers had all seen his photograph in the newspapers before picking him out in the identity parade.

When, at last, the parade was finally over, Morrison was formally charged with murder. His only response was, 'All that I can say is that it is a lie.'

A police visit to his lodgings in York Road, Lambeth, produced further clothing belonging to Morrison. Inside the lining of his bowler hat was a cloakroom ticket relating to a parcel left at St Mary's railway station in Whitechapel, now known as Aldgate East. It had been deposited by a man answering Morrison's description, but giving the name of Bandman. The contents proved to be a fully loaded revolver and a box of forty-four cartridges. The shape of the gun had been disguised by being wrapped in a towel before the brown paper was applied. The parcel had been handed in at eleven o'clock on New Year's Day, only eight hours after the murder.

Some indication of the nature of the eventual trial came from an incident during a preliminary hearing at a police court held on 25 January.

The prosecution produced a witness whom they clearly regarded as a 'trump card'. This was an eighteen-year-old girl named Eva Flitterman. She was employed in the clothing industry as a tailoress and lived with her mother at 18 Thrawl Street, Spitalfields, her father having died in early December. Miss Flitterman spoke very little English and use was made of someone who had come to the court in connection with another case. The interpreter proved to be a cause of great complaint and argument, however, since the defendant alleged that he not only translated but altered and augmented what the girl said.

The court did, however, learn from Eva that, at about the end of December, she had been introduced to Morrison by a man called Issy. She spent a couple of hours with Morrison and met him on four or five further occasions; he then asked her to marry him. During these meetings she saw him wearing a watch and chain. Attached to the chain was a £5 piece. In response to questioning, she told the court that she knew that it was a £5 piece because it was just like the one that her father had. If true, this was indeed a damning piece of evidence. Unfortunately for the prosecution, the very next day Miss Flitterman appeared once more in the witness-box, this time to admit that she had made a mistake. On her way home after the previous day's hearing, she had been told by her mother that the coin on her father's watch was a £2 piece not a £5 piece.

Counsel for the Crown, clearly angered and feeling no doubt that he had been made to look foolish, spoke to the presiding magistrate about perjury charges. The magistrate, having more sense, considered such action wholly unjustified. Miss Flitterman, he said, had simply made a mistake; she probably had no idea what a £5 piece looked like.

On 6 March 1911 Steinie Morrison came before Mr Justice Darling at the Central Criminal Court to face a charge of wilful murder. Mr R.D. Muir appeared for the Crown, Mr E. Abinger for the defendant. Almost all the witnesses, for both sides, were East European Jews. Their understanding of the English language was variable and frequently ideosyncratic. The one thing that they all had in common was complete ignorance of English court procedure. These two factors were to produce not a little excitement and a fair amount of hilarity.

Mr Abinger, in particular, found on numerous occasions that his attempts to cross-examine witnesses led him into a veritable quagmire of misunderstanding. On at least one occasion he had to be rescued by the learned judge gently pointing out to the witness,

'You are not supposed to be asking counsel questions, you are supposed to answer his.'

Another witness, faced by a series of questions which to him did not seem to be relevant, declared:

'What are you asking me that for? What has that got to do with anything? If all you are going to do is ask me silly questions I'm going home.'

Mr Henry Hermilin seemed to counsel to be over-fond of answering his questions with the phrase 'a couple of times'.

'How many times do you understand "a couple of times" to be?'

'It can be ten times, it can be more.'

Mr Abinger, trying to discredit one witness by implying that she allowed her lodging-house to be used by prostitutes, asked,

'Where did you get your fur coat?'

'How dare you ask me such a question?' was the instant response. 'What's it got to do with you? Do I ask you where your wife got her fur coat from?'

There was also Mrs Nellie Deitch who spoke for many a married woman faced by an uncomprehending male.

'My husband is a gas-fitter.'

'I see. And what are you?'

'What am I? I am a woman of course.'

'Yes, I can see that, but what is your occupation?'

'My occupation? That is a fine question to ask me. I am at home in the house. Looking after my children. Looking after the business. We have a gas-fitting shop and I look after it while my husband does the work outside.'

It quickly became apparent in the trial that, between the stream of witnesses on the one hand and the lawyers and court officials on the other, there stretched a vast, almost unbridgeable social gulf. As the court heard from witness after witness of the way these people lived and of their social attitudes, counsel were by no means always sure whether the witnesses were serious or were mocking the court.

They heard from Solomon Beron, the murdered man's brother. Questioned, he disclosed that he lived in a common lodging-house for 7d a night and spent about 1s a day on meals at the Warsaw Restaurant. When first appearing in the witness-box he had declared himself to be 'a gentleman of independent means'.

To Mr Abinger these strange people were a source of almost total bafflement, to Mr Justice Darling one of endless fascination. His interest and sympathy towards them was obvious as he gently questioned them about their lives.

There was, in particular, sixteen-year-old Jack Taw. In response to His Lordship's questions he explained that he had come to England three years ago when he was only thirteen. He originated in Galicia in Austria-Hungary, his father was dead and he had travelled alone to England. He had known no one in this country when he arrived and lived now by working occasionally as a waiter at the Warsaw Restaurant, being paid sometimes 1s, sometimes 1s-6d a day.

In spite of all the difficulties and complications the prosecution steadily built up their case. It was entirely circumstantial but it all fitted neatly together. They were able to show, for instance, that, for a period of seven weeks in the autumn of 1910, Morrison had been employed as a baker's roundsman by a Mr Pithers who owned a bakery in Lavender Hill, in the vicinity of Clapham Common. He therefore knew the area well.

As witness followed witness, each testifying to having seen the victim and accused together on the night of Beron's murder, so the minds of the jury became more and more certain of Morrison's guilt. It was the sheer accumulation of evidence that did it. Defence counsel was able to pick holes in individual accounts but not in the accumulated mass.

When, at last, it became time for the case to be put for the defence, Mr Abinger had more trouble with witnesses, this time with his own, some of whom proved to be of very dubious value.

According to Morrison, the events of that fatal evening were very different to those portrayed by the prosecution. He claimed that he went to the Warsaw Restaurant at about eight o'clock but left at 8.30 and went to the Shoreditch Empire. He purchased a seat for 1s-6d and stayed there until after eleven. At the end of the show he returned to the restaurant where he had a cup of tea and a piece of cake. He once more left at a quarter to twelve, returned to his lodgings in Newark Street and remained there the rest of the night. As for seeing Beron, after leaving the restaurant he walked along Whitechapel Road until he came to the corner of Cambridge Heath Road and then crossed into Sidney Street. As he turned the corner into Sidney Street he heard someone call out, 'Bonsoir, Monsieur'. When he looked round, he saw Beron standing on the other side of the road with a tall man. In reply to questions, Morrison was unable to remember any of the acts that he had seen at the music hall.

In support of Morrison's story, defence counsel first produced his landlords Mr and Mrs Zimmerman. They told the court that Morrison had returned home slightly after midnight and went to bed. Mr Zimmerman had then locked and bolted the front door before they too retired for the night. They both claimed that, while it was perfectly true that Morrison had a key and could have let himself out and then in again, the bolt on the door was very stiff and noisy. As they slept in the room next to the front hall and were both light sleepers they would have been woken by any attempt to draw the bolt.

Prosecution counsel at this point commented that, given his experience, Morrison should have had no difficulty in getting in and out of a house without waking the inhabitants. Mr Abinger complained that Mr Muir was making his client sound like a burglar. The learned judge remarked that he did, after all, have two convictions for burglary.

Two teenage girls, Esther and Jane Brodsky, then took their turns in the witness-box. They swore that, on the evening in question, they too went to the Shoreditch Empire. They arrived at the theatre at nine o'clock, purchased two 1s seats and, while watching the show, saw Morrison seated nearby. In response to questioning the only act that either of them could recollect seeing was Harry Champion singing 'Ginger, You're Barmy'.

In response to this claim, the prosecution produced the assistant manager of the theatre. He testified that, on the evening of 31 December, there were only two rows of seats priced at 1s and one row at 1s-6d. All the remaining seats in the music hall were priced at 1s-9d. He said that he had been on duty that evening and told the court that all the 1s-9ds were booked-up by five o'clock in the afternoon. He declared that people began queuing for the remaining seats at seven o'clock and that by 7.15 p.m. there were already more people queuing than there were seats available. When the doors opened at 8.30 all thirty unbooked seats were sold within a few minutes. No one turning up at nine o'clock could possibly have obtained a seat. Harry Champion sang 'Ginger, You're Barmy' every night.

There was a more unusual outbreak of courtroom drama when, during the closing speech for the defence, Solomon Beron was seen to become more and more excited. He suddenly leapt to his feet, ran to the front of the court, waved his fist at Mr Abinger and shouted,

'He is my brother's murderer and you are going to get him off.'

With a great deal of difficulty police officers overpowered him and dragged him, still shouting, from the court. He was taken to a mental asylum.

At the end of an exhausting nine-day trial the jury took only thirty-five minutes to decide upon a 'Guilty' verdict. Mr Justice Darling then donned his black cap and began the traditional speech leading to the death sentence.

Steinie Morrison, you have been found guilty, after a long, careful and most patient investigation, of the crime of wilful murder.

Undoubtedly your case was supported by evidence demonstrably false. I am sure that that did not unduly weigh with the jury and that they have convicted you upon the strength of the evidence for the prosecution and upon that alone.

My one duty is to pass the judgement which the law awards; it is that you be taken hence to the prison from whence you came; that you be taken thence to a place of lawful execution; that you be there hanged by the neck until your body is dead and may the Lord have mercy on your soul.

The Times, in its comments on the case, proved to be much less sensible and understanding than Mr Justice Darling of the poor refugees in the East End.

> Justice has overtaken him at last, and the country will be rid of a cold-blooded assassin and a most undesirable alien. The case against him proved to be overwhelming.
>
> In the mind of the public at large the story of this long trial will confirm very strongly the impression so prevalent of late – that the East End of London counts among its population a large number of very dangerous, very reckless and very noxious people, chiefly immigrants from the Eastern and South Eastern countries of Europe. The second impression will be that these people add to the difficulties of the situation by their extreme untrustworthiness, since lying, especially in the witness-box, appears to be their natural language.

The leader-writers of *The Times* might, perhaps, have noted that, without the willing co-operation of 'these people', Morrison would never have been caught, let alone convicted.

It had been noticeable in Mr Justice Darling's closing speech that, while he had kept to much of the standard formula, he had not personally endorsed the verdict of the jury. He may well have felt that Morrison was guilty but that the prosecution had failed to prove it. The neat cobweb of circumstantial evidence did not, by any means, amount to a strong net of proven fact.

This obvious opinion of the judge was almost certainly one of the aspects of the case that led the Home Secretary, Mr Churchill, to reprieve the death sentence. Morrison, however, faced by the prospect of spending the rest of his life confined to a prison-cell became ever more violent and then, with great determination, deliberately starved himself to death in January 1921.

There were those at the time (and since) who have been less than satisfied of Morrison's guilt, preferring to see him as a pawn in an anarchist conspiracy. Could he have been employed to befriend Beron and then to lure him to the open spaces of Clapham Common where he could be punished for a suspected betrayal?

Others, however, argue that when a known criminal – and Morrison was one – carefully befriends a man known to carry large sums of money on his person, and that man is then murdered and robbed, a theory of anarchist conspiracy is scarcely necessary. It is highly unlikely that the full truth will ever be known. Certainly there are aspects of the police story that are less than convincing.

There is, for instance, the manner of Beron's death. According to the official explanation Morrison, having successfully lured the unsuspecting Beron to a lonely spot, promptly attacked him without warning. That is a perfectly reasonable supposition. But what was the nature of the attack? Morrison produces an iron bar and rains no less than eight violent blows on his victim's head, an attack which not only kills him but effectively destroys a large part of the man's head and face. Then, as his victim lies dead at his feet, Morrison puts the murder weapon to one side, draws a knife and carries out a second attack, during the course of which he stabs the already dead man five times and accidentally slashes his victim's face in the process. Alternatively, of course, he could have attacked first with the knife and only used the iron bar when Beron had already been stabbed to death.

Either way it does not sound plausible. Surely it is much more likely that the unfortunate Beron was attacked and killed by at least two men, one using a knife and one the iron bar? So who was the second man?

The police would no doubt point to the mysterious man whom Morrison was supposed to have met at Kennington and who travelled with him to Finsbury Park. But, if that were true, how did the second killer manage to reach the Oval as quickly as, if not quicker than, Morrison? The official account has Morrison crossing Clapham Common by the shortest possible route and then almost immediately taking a cab to Kennington. It is difficult to see how anyone could have performed that journey, in the middle of the night, in less time. And yet, when Morrison reached Kennington he once more met up with his accomplice without any delay. All very curious.

In any case, that story of the third cab journey is by no means convincing. It was based on an identification by a cab-driver who had already seen a photograph of Morrison and who had been offered a reward for information. The reported behaviour of Morrison is also strange. Having apparently been decisive all night he is suddenly unable to decide whether or not to take a cab! And Finsbury Park is a long way removed from the normal hunting-ground of both Morrison and his alleged anarchist friends.

On the other hand, the argument that Morrison cultivated the friendship of Beron at the instigation of the anarchists, with the specific intention of luring him to his death, ignores the fact that he began doing so at least a month before the Houndsditch murders.

According to some reports, after his conviction Morrison claimed that he had been unable to give a true account of his movements on that New Year's night because he had been taking part in a bank robbery. If that were true it would account also for the gun that he deposited shortly afterwards. Contemporary newspapers have no reports of a bank robbery taking place at that time.

All things considered the only surprising thing about the case and its scope for speculation is that no one has, as yet, come up with the theory that Morrison was Peter the Painter.

THE DOCTOR'S
HOUSE

THE DOCTOR'S HOUSE

An Englishman's home is his castle. But who knows what goes on behind the walls of a castle? As we walk along a street, looking at the houses, what can we know of life within them? We see their front gardens, perhaps admire their roses. We see their curtains and wonder at their strange tastes. But of the life within, behind that thin brick facade, we can only guess. Occasionally however, just occasionally, truly dramatic events occur. When that happens private life becomes public knowledge. We can all be amazed, can all say – how different to the life within our own dear homes!

The Kent town of Faversham is one of the nicest and most picturesque towns in England. It has a long and colourful history during which it contributed ships to fight the Armada. It then had the good fortune to sleep quietly through the worst of the Industrial Revolution. As a result it has retained much of its character and many of its oldest and most beautiful houses.

In delightfully sinuous West Street, not far from the market place, tucked between the rambling medieval bulk of the Sun public-house and a nineteenth-century shop-front full of rolls of wallpaper, stands number 12.

Number 12 West Street is a Georgian house. The description 'Georgian house' usually conjures up a picture of a grand, imposing building with an elegant, impressive front door. But number 12 is not like that at all. It is a small house, the front door opening straight onto the street. Either side of the unpretentious door there is room for just one window. Above, the pattern is much the same; a small window in the centre, flanked by larger windows on either side. Above the

101

brick facade can be seen a row of attic windows.

Towards the end of the nineteenth century this was a doctor's house, the home of Dr Lyddon. A doctor's house in a small, quiet town in late Victorian England, what could be more respectable than that? And yet, behind those walls there was drink, drugs, violence and sudden death.

Dr William Reeks Lyddon first began to practise medicine in Faversham in 1878. He continued to do so for almost twelve years, apparently to everyone's satisfaction. Certainly many of his patients continued to use his services and exhibit loyalty towards him even when, from 1889 onwards, his personal problems caused him to be a less than perfect general practitioner.

By 1890 he was forty-four years old and a widower. His father had been Collector of Taxes for Canterbury and, after the death of his mother, had married again. This second marriage also produced a son, Charles, who was Dr Lyddon's junior by some sixteen years. Charles Lyddon also showed an interest in medicine. After the necessary period of study he passed the first examination of the College of Surgeons, also the first and second examinations of the College of Physicians. He failed for some unknown reason to complete his studies. While he never became a doctor, however, he did qualify as a dispenser and it was in that capacity that, in 1878, he began to assist his half-brother in his practice. Charles continued to live with his parents in Canterbury, commuting between there and Faversham, a distance of eight miles. According to his own account Dr Lyddon agreed to pay him £50 a year for his services, but omitted to do so. Indeed, the doctor borrowed money from him.

At that time his father was paying him an allowance of between £200 and £300 a year, a comfortable income in those days. He had, therefore, no need to be too concerned at his lack of salary. In 1886 this all changed. His father died, leaving him nothing. An uncle died, leaving him a legacy worth £270, together with some furniture and plate, but, apart from a small allowance from his mother, he now had no regular income.

Soon after the death of Mr Lyddon his wife and son moved to Faversham where they set up house with the doctor. It was one of those family arrangements that seem, at the time, to make perfect sense. Dr Lyddon had lost his wife and needed someone to look after the house. Mrs Lyddon could do that for him. Charles Lyddon was already working for him and would be much more valuable living-in than travelling to and fro from Canterbury. In common with many such arrangements it proved to be considerably less than perfect in practice.

If there was one single cause of all the trouble that was to come to 12 West Street it was, without any doubt at all, drink. Both William and Charles drank whisky to excess. When they did so they became quarrelsome and, certainly in the case of Charles, violent. It might not have been so serious had Mrs Lyddon had more sense. But she seems to have found it quite possible to be both quarrelsome and violent even without the use of alcohol.

In spite of the dangerously volatile atmosphere in the house the three members of the Lyddon family managed to live together for two or three years without any serious disturbance. From time to time the two men would become drunk, would quarrel over money and Charles would threaten violence. But somehow it was contained, they would sleep it off and the outside world would know little of it. When sober the two half-brothers appeared to get on well with one another, were even affectionate. The trouble was that they were not sober often enough.

In the spring of 1889 Dr Lyddon developed a stomach ulcer which needed surgery. Today, such an operation would seem routine, at any rate to the medical world. In 1889 such an operation was perilous, a fact that William Lyddon, a doctor, could not fail to know. When, therefore, his half-brother asked for a legally written deed to safeguard his interests, in the distinctly possible event of the doctor's death, there seemed to be no good reason to refuse.

A Whitstable solicitor, Mr John Wiggins, was consulted by the two brothers, but the deed was drawn up by a different solicitor, Mr Frederick Gibson of Sittingbourne, in accordance with the sole instructions of Charles Lyddon. Mr Gibson, who seems to have been a fair-minded man, recommended that William Lyddon have his own solicitor but this was not done. Mr Gibson never saw Dr Lyddon.

The deed of assignment went considerably further than could have been expected. In effect, it not only guaranteed Charles the outstanding twelve years' unpaid wages, plus various sums allegedly loaned during that period, it also placed the doctor totally at the mercy of his half-brother. In theory, whenever he chose, Charles Lyddon could call for a complete payment of the debt. If it were not immediately forthcoming he could seize everything that the doctor owned as settlement. The wording bound Dr Lyddon 'absolutely to sell & assign to Charles Lyddon all his interests and goodwill in the practice, the debts, stock-in-trade, horses, carriages, furniture, plate & effects'.

Dr Lyddon was in St Thomas's Hospital for over two months. He did not, however, die and in August 1889 returned to Faversham once more to take up his medical practice.

He had been under the impression that the deed of assignment had been drawn up solely to cover the eventuality of his death in hospital. Charles Lyddon saw matters differently. Shortly after it had been signed and witnessed by a neighbour, Richard Dunn, he had read it to his coachman, George Amos. 'I am master of everything now,' he said. He was less than sober at the time but it indicated his view. Asked to hand over or destroy the now unnecessary document, he refused. From that time on he began to behave as if he were, indeed, master of everything.

With the return to Faversham of the now recovered Dr Lyddon a new character enters our story. It must be understood that there were several employees attached to the Lyddon household. Firstly, there was Mrs Hunt; she came in three or four times a week to clean and also to collect and, in due course, return the laundry. Then there was George Amos, employed as a coachman, who eventually left, to be replaced by a man called Ford. There was also Henry Lyons who helped in the stables. But all these people went off to their own homes at the end of the day. They could have had, therefore, only occasional glimpses of the real life of the house.

Early in August 1889, however, Charles Naylor joined the household as page-boy and it is through his eyes that we see much of what happened in that strange place over the next five months. He was a local lad, aged just fifteen. While the Lyddons called him a 'page-boy' his duties were considerably more extensive than that title might infer. He looked after the surgery and kept it clean; he answered the door. He learnt dispensing. And, since there were no female servants in the house, he assisted Mrs Lyddon in cooking, making the beds, etc., plus anything else that might occur to any member of the family. He conducted all these varying occupations in good humour and to the best of his ability.

Over the next two or three months the situation at 12 West Street rapidly deteriorated. This cannot have been helped by the fact that Dr Lyddon had, by now, developed an addiction to morphia. At that time morphia was one of the very few pain-killers available to the medical profession. It was accordingly used extensively both inside and outside hospital. It is a drug that is notoriously addictive. For someone like William Lyddon, who required it for his surgery, addiction was not only easy to acquire but also extremely difficult to banish.

The behaviour of his half-brother did not help. From then onwards the household rows became increasingly common, increasingly violent and increasingly public. According to Charles Naylor they invariably began with drinking bouts. There then came arguments about money, claims that the doctor was ruining the practice by his drug-taking and threats to throw him out of the house.

George Amos was witness to many of these quarrels. On one occasion he saw Charles punch his brother in the face, knocking him down and giving him a black eye. Nor was Charles the only one involved. On another occasion Amos saw Mrs Lyddon hit the doctor with a big stick, causing a massive bruise on the arm.

The night following that incident, while he was working in the stables, Charles called out to Amos, telling him to go to the doctor and take care of him because he was drunk and delirious. The coachman went upstairs. He found Dr Lyddon in bed, neither drunk nor delirious. Indeed, if anyone was drunk, it was Charles, who tried repeatedly to strike the man as he lay in bed. Amos prevented him from doing so. Charles then turned his violence on Amos, threatening to murder him. Amos, however, was not only sober but also stronger and fitter. During the fight that followed it was Charles who was knocked down.

On yet another occasion, hearing a great commotion upstairs, Amos went up to the doctor's bedroom. He found the doctor cowering on the floor while his brother stood over him, accusing him of having whisky in his room. Declaring his intention of finding it, Charles began to pull everything out of the wardrobe and cupboards, throwing the contents all around the room. Finding locked drawers he went out and came back with a chisel which he used to force them open. When one small drawer proved especially stubborn, he obtained a larger chisel and smashed it open. The drawer contained Dr Lyddon's small mementos of his dead wife. Charles Lyddon proceeded to tear them from the drawer, throwing them around. To the doctor's pleas to stop, he cried 'Oh b— your wife.' Seeing the state that Charles Lyddon was in, Amos chose to stay the night in the doctor's room. During the course of the night Charles again came back to search for whisky, once again throwing things about the room, including the toilet set from the dressing-table.

George Amos was not the only witness to these outbursts of violence. Henry Lyons was called from the stables into the house by Mrs Lyddon. She told him to strap Dr Lyddon to a kitchen chair because, she said, he was delirious. The doctor said to him, 'They will not let me have a moment's peace.' He began to get up out of his chair. As he did so Mrs Lyddon struck him on the arm and Charles punched him in the face. The doctor was quite clearly not delirious.

One Saturday evening in September Inspector Fowle, of the local constabulary, met Charles Naylor in the street. Told that he was on his way to the police station in search of help, the inspector went to the house with the young lad. He found Charles Lyddon sitting by the dining-room door with a double-barrelled shotgun across his knee. Dr Lyddon told the inspector, 'My brother is threatening me with a gun and I cannot go into the surgery to do my business.' The reply from Charles was, 'Yes, and if you come near me I will use it.' At the quiet insistence of the inspector, and not without argument, he eventually put the gun down, saying that they were only blank cartridges anyway. As the doctor stepped past him into the dining-room and began to say something, Charles struck him in the stomach. 'Your breath stinks,' he said, 'and I don't want it in my mouth.' The doctor then made his way into the surgery. The police officer meanwhile remained in the dining-room with Charles Lyddon, telling him exactly what he thought of him and warning him never again to threaten anyone with a gun. Charles had quite clearly been drinking.

During September 1890 an old medical friend of Dr Lyddon, Dr William Hill, while staying in the Faversham area called in to see him. He found his friend ill with catarrhal pneumonia. The sick man's room was untidy, the bed had not been made and the slops were unemptied. Dr Hill made a number of visits to the house. Being extremely doubtful as to whether proper food was being provided for the patient he took food in himself. He supplied Brands Essence and, later, a chicken. As only a short-term visitor to the area, there was a limit to what he could do. He did, however, insist that Charles Lyddon call in a local doctor to attend to his brother who was, by now, seriously ill.

On 30 September, in response to Dr Hill's urging, a Faversham doctor, Dr Boswell, received a request from Charles to attend his sick brother. Dr Boswell, who had already been fully briefed by Dr Hill, promised to visit the patient at nine o'clock that same evening. Upon reaching the house he rang the front-door bell. After some delay, the door was opened by Charles Naylor. The doctor asked to see Charles Lyddon. Told by Naylor that Mr Lyddon was asleep, he demanded that he be woken up; he had called by appointment and Mr Lyddon was responsible for the welfare of his brother. The boy explained that

Mr Lyddon was in no state to see anyone. He did, however, admit the doctor to the house.

Dr Boswell was led up the stairs where he found Charles Lyddon lying on the landing, so drunk as to be speechless. Nearby was a young woman, also hopelessly drunk. Entering the sick man's bedroom, he found him very ill indeed. He was dirty and neglected. The bed had not been made. Young Naylor appearing to be the only member of the household not drunk, the doctor questioned him. 'What nourishment has the patient been given today?' The answer was that the sick man had been given only a glass of beer and a cup of tea. 'Exactly who is responsible for nursing him?' He was informed that the nurse was the young woman whom he had just seen, drunk on the landing.

The doctor, both extremely concerned and very angry, did what he could to help the sick man and then returned to his own surgery where he met Dr Hill. The two medical colleagues discussed the situation and concluded that William Lyddon would most certainly die if he were left in the house under the tender ministrations of his brother. He was in urgent need of proper medical care and skilled nursing.

Early the next morning Dr Boswell returned to West Street where he told Charles Lyddon, who was by now relatively sober, that he would not treat the patient unless he were removed to the Cottage Hospital. After some argument this was eventually agreed. Asked, 'Do you think my brother is going to get better?' Dr Boswell retorted, 'I hope so, but it is no thanks to you that he is not dead now.' As preparations were being made for the transfer of the sick man to hospital Dr Lyddon gave Naylor £1-5s-6d, asking him to look after it for him, as he said, 'Charles takes money out of my pockets.'

Throughout his first week in hospital Dr Lyddon was delirious but then, thanks to careful nursing, gradually recovered. During his stay he told Dr Boswell the story of his period in St Thomas's Hospital and of 'the deed of assignment'. He remained in the Cottage Hospital until 26 October when he was removed by Charles Lyddon against medical advice. Dr Lyddon explained to his fellow doctor that he had received letters from his half-brother. He did not wish to leave hospital but if he did not go he would have to suffer for it later. 'Charles will stop at nothing,' he said.

The return of Dr Lyddon from hospital soon resulted in further disturbances in West Street. On several occasions the police were called, sometimes by one brother, sometimes by the other. Charles developed a fondness for showing bunches of keys, saying that he was master of the house, and frequently urged the police to throw his brother out. Regarding it as a purely domestic matter the police declined to take any such action. Having failed to get any support from the police, Charles visited the Sittingbourne solicitor, Mr Gibson, complaining about his brother, demanding that the deed of assignment be used and that his brother be forced from the house. Mr Gibson advised against any such action.

On Thursday, 20 November, Naylor overheard Charles complaining to his mother that the doctor had turned two patients out of the surgery. He declared that the doctor would ruin the practice.

Having failed to persuade Mr Gibson to force the doctor out of the house, Charles decided to try a different solicitor. He telephoned a Mr Wiggins. Upon his arrival there was a long discussion in the drawing-room. Twice during that conference Dr Lyddon called Naylor and told him to fetch a solicitor to represent him. On the first occasion he asked for a Mr Tassell and on the second for a Mr Johnson. On neither occasion did Naylor do anything, having been given strict instructions, in advance, by Charles not to do so. When the lad told Charles that he had been asked by the doctor to go for Mr Tassell, but that he had not done so, Mr Lyddon said to him, 'No, don't you go. If you do, I shall know how to deal with you.' Mr Wiggins was, in fact, no more prepared to force Dr Lyddon out of the house than Mr Gibson had been. After a long discussion he left to consider what recommendations he could make for an amicable settlement.

The departure of the solicitor, without any apparent change in the situation, was the signal for a new outburst of noisy argument. Dr Lyddon endeavoured to get away from his half-brother by moving to the dining-room, but was immediately followed there by both Charles and Mrs Lyddon who was just as violently quarrelsome as her son.

After some time Mrs Lyddon emerged from the dining-room and went upstairs to her room where she began dressing to go out. Dr Lyddon moved back into the drawing-room, sat down in an armchair and declared that he would not go. He had obviously been drinking but was by no means drunk. His brother shouted, 'You will either go to Herne Bay or go out of the house.'

The trap was quickly got ready and Dr Lyddon was bundled into it where he was joined by his stepmother. Charles then climbed into the driving-seat and drove them to the railway station.

At about five o'clock that afternoon Ronald McDonald, a Herne Bay cabinet-maker, came across a man whom he later learned was Dr Lyddon. The man was in Station Road, Herne Bay and was reeling about the road as if he were drunk. He caught hold of one of the iron posts supporting a shop-blind, swung round and fell to his knees. He lay in a most peculiar manner, his forehead and knees on the ground but with his legs in the air. Mr McDonald went over to help.

'Allow me to lend you a hand, brother,' he said.

'I am alright,' came the reply. 'I only want another glass.' At this point, Mr Weatherly also came upon the scene and, each man taking an arm, they helped him to his feet.

'Where do you live?' asked Mr McDonald.

'Marine Terrace.'

Seeing a woman standing nearby, Mr McDonald asked her,

'Do you know him?'

'He is my son,' she said, 'one of the leading doctors in Faversham, do help him.'

'Gladly, Ma'am.'

The two men assisted him to 1 Marine Terrace, a boarding-house run by a Mrs Sarah Stuart. The Lyddon family were no strangers to Mrs Stuart, having stayed with her on several occasions. She was well aware that all the family were over-fond of drink, but had never before seen Dr Lyddon drunk. She thought his behaviour very strange. At first she believed him to be drunk but he did not really behave like a drunken man. Although he seemed to have no control of his legs, he talked sensibly. Mrs Lyddon just said that he had been drinking but the landlady was not convinced and called in her own, highly qualified, doctor. Faced by the patient's complete refusal to co-operate, he was unable to come to any conclusions. Dr Lyddon declined to show his tongue or even allow his pulse to be taken.

He continued to behave in a very odd manner, having to be helped to bed, Mrs Stuart's son undressing him. Still concerned and puzzled by his condition, Mrs Stuart remained close by him all night. Throughout the night he was restless, constantly tossing about and groaning. The next morning he was violently sick.

Later that day, Friday 21st, Charles arrived with a carriage, apparently with the intention of taking his half-brother back with him to Faversham. Dr Lyddon, who had so strongly resisted coming to Herne Bay, now refused to leave it. After the inevitable argument Charles returned to Faversham on his own, it having been agreed that the doctor should stay at Herne Bay for the weekend.

Over the next few days he slowly recovered. On the Monday

morning, Mrs Stuart took him up a breakfast of tea and toast at eight o'clock. At ten, when he had a basin of milk, Mrs Stuart asked him how he was. He placed his hands on his sides, complaining of shooting-pains and said he couldn't understand it.

At eleven o'clock that morning Charles Lyddon once more arrived with the carriage. He stayed at Marine Terrace for lunch and during the course of conversation explained to Mrs Stuart that the doctor was in the habit of taking drugs. On Dr Lyddon's first night at her house Mrs Stuart had searched his clothes in an attempt to find his tobacco. She had found no trace of drugs or indeed of tobacco.

Soon after midday on 24 November Dr Lyddon arrived back at Faversham. He was clearly a great deal better than when he went away. Not having had any lunch, Naylor obtained for him some raw, minced steak which he had, washed down with a glass of stout. That was at 1.30. While he was eating it his half-brother sat in an armchair nearby. The two men appeared to be on very good terms. Between four and five the doctor went out to visit his patients, returning between six and seven.

During the evening two patients called to see him, Mrs Waters and Frank Sherlock. Mr Sherlock, who was the fly-driver for the Ship Hotel, called at 8.50 p.m. Upon arrival at the house, he asked to see the doctor and was shown by Naylor into the surgery. Shortly afterwards he was joined by Dr Lyddon. In a reversal of the usual procedure, Sherlock asked the doctor how he was feeling and was told 'very much better'. Mr Sherlock said that he had come to pay his bill but was told that it was not yet ready. He therefore left, saying that he would call back later that week. The doctor seemed to Mr Sherlock to be both sober and healthy.

Not long after the departure of Mr Sherlock the doctor asked Naylor to go out for some milk. When he returned Dr Lyddon gave him careful instructions for the preparation of medicines for his patients. He then wrote out the labels for the bottles and between nine and ten Naylor was sent out to deliver them to the respective patients. At this time the doctor appeared to have consumed some alcohol but was still reasonably sober.

The boy returned to the house at 10.15 p.m. According to Charles Lyddon, during the period that Naylor was out of the house a great deal had been happening. It began when Charles walked into the drawing-room, where the doctor was seated, and asked, 'Well Crewe, how have you got on?' This led to a complaint from the doctor that he had 'nearly broken my neck, thanks to that beastly trap, which I have to use. Why can't I have a new one?' His half-brother replied that he could have a new trap when the debts had been paid off and not before. By now both men had been at the whisky bottle. As the alcohol continued to flow, so the quarrel grew. The two brothers began to wander from room to room, carrying the whisky bottles with them, arguing all the time.

Yet, when Naylor returned from his errand, he heard no row. The doctor was in Mrs Lyddon's room, asleep on her couch. Naylor went downstairs and through to the kitchen. He had been there about half an hour when Charles Lyddon came downstairs and told him to go to the police station for Inspector Fowle. He did as he was told, but the inspector was out. Only P.C. Stone was on duty. Naylor returned to the house and reported to his employer. He was immediately ordered to go back to the police station and ask P.C. Stone if he would come to the house. At the police station he was told by P.C Stone, who no doubt regarded the Lyddon family as a confounded nuisance, that he could not leave the station unattended. Once more the boy returned to West Street alone. Twice more the boy journeyed to and from the police station until, after his fourth visit, he found Inspector Fowle.

When, at last, the inspector arrived upon the scene he demanded to know what on earth was the matter.

'This deed of assignment,' said Charles. 'You know all about it? I want my brother to leave the house.'

'Where is he?' asked the inspector.

'Upstairs on the couch.'

'If he is upstairs and comfortable, the best thing you can do is to go to bed yourself.'

Charles was far from satisfied by this sensible advice and insisted that the police officer force his half-brother out of the house. This the inspector resolutely refused to do, pointing out that it was a freezing cold night and that there was nowhere else for the doctor to go.

'My brother is in the habit of taking drugs and I might be accused of it,' he was told.

Mrs Lyddon intervened:

'Yours is very kind advice sir,' she said. 'And I am ashamed of Mr Lyddon to want to turn the doctor out, as he is laying very ill and not fit to be turned out.'

But still Charles insisted on his brother being expelled from the house:

'Mr Wiggins wants him out,' he said.

'You are not bound to do what Mr Wiggins tells you,' replied the inspector. He then once more told them to go to bed and left.

For a while peace descended on 12 West Street but it was not to last. According to Charles, he wrote a few letters, then went upstairs with the intention of going to bed. When he reached the top of the stairs he looked into his brother's room to see if he was asleep. He was not and attempts on the part of Charles to persuade him to do so rapidly led to renewed arguments, ostensibly about the 'beastly trap'. From what we know of Charles Lyddon, however, this account of events seems highly unlikely. It is much more probable that he had been drinking again and was ready for yet another argument. At any rate there was soon a full-scale row, with Mrs Lyddon also heavily involved.

When at 11.50 p.m. Naylor, after having extinguished all the lights on the ground floor as was the usual custom, mounted the stairs ready for bed, he heard Mrs Lyddon say, 'Don't hit him in the face.' He also heard the doctor call out, 'Oh. Joe, Joe, you blackguard.' The doctor, who had been in his stepmother's room, moved across into his own room in an attempt to get away, but the other two followed him.

Mrs Lyddon declared that he needed horse-whipping to keep him away from drugs. Her son told Naylor, 'Go and get me the tanning whip,' but the boy made no attempt to do so. Mrs Lyddon then went up to the doctor, striking him three times on the shoulder with her fist. Not satisfied with that she seized a wooden bonnet-stand, declaring her intention to 'crack his head open'. Charles, in a rare moment of sense, prevented her from doing so.

Dr Lyddon, with the air of a man determined to go to bed, removed his coat and threw it on a chair. He then took off his waistcoat which he tossed onto the bottom of the bed. It was at this point that Charles thought up a new way of humiliating his half-brother. He told him that he would have to sleep in the lumber-room. This led, quite understandably, to further heated argument. After a great deal of shouting Naylor suggested to the doctor that he had better do as they said, 'for the sake of peace and quiet'. He then took hold of the man's arm and gently led him through to the little-room, as they usually called it. By now the doctor was very drunk indeed, staggering about. Charles had also consumed far too much whisky but was not in such a bad state as his half-brother.

While there was some furniture in the lumber-room, there was no bedding. Directed by Charles, Naylor collected a blanket and sheet from the doctor's room. These he carried into the lumber-room, together with a lighted candle, there being no other means of lighting in there. The room was situated immediately above the kitchen and there was a chimney-stack which ran up the side of the room, carrying smoke from the downstairs fires. This, according to Charles, prevented the room from becoming too cold although he, of course, had never slept there.

Faced by a mixture of coaxing from the boy and threats from the other two, the doctor entered the little-room, taking his coat with him. The candle was removed, leaving him in total darkness, the door closed and then securely locked. Charles carefully pocketed the keys.

In Mrs Lyddon's room, Naylor had seen a bottle of whisky about a third full, together with a tumbler. Knowing his employer well, he mentioned it to Charles, asking him if he wanted it. 'Yes,' was the unsurprising answer, 'you had better get it.' Naylor did so, placing the bottle on the chest of drawers. The tumbler was left in Mrs Lyddon's room.

Naylor, who had a room in the attic but, in practice, usually shared with the doctor, was told by Charles to sleep in his bed that night. The boy got into bed first, lying close to the wall. Charles then climbed in, still wearing his trousers, a by no means unusual state of affairs.

At about 7.30 the next morning Charles was awoken by the arrival of the postman. He got out of bed and, not having bothered to undress the night before, went straight downstairs to read the letters. They included a long letter from Mr Wiggins, giving suggestions for a settlement of the money dispute between the two brothers.

By this time Naylor had also been woken up by activity in the street below. As he lay there in bed he saw a bunch of keys lying alongside him. Shortly afterwards, when Charles returned, telling the lad to get up, Naylor drew his attention to the bunch of keys. Charles picked them up, saying that he was going to see how his brother was. The boy was, by now, out of bed, dressing. Having got his clothes on he descended the stairs and set about lighting the kitchen fire.

As Charles passed through his mother's room she was still fast asleep. He took the bunch of keys out of his pocket, selected the correct one and unlocked the door of the lumber-room. He opened the door and looked in at his half-brother. The man lay on his back, snoring noisily. The bedding, together with his coat and some other clothing, lay on top of him. According to Charles he saw nothing about his brother's condition to alarm him. The man's breathing was more laboured than normal but he had seen him like it many times before.

Mrs Lyddon was now also awake. She joined her son and talked of getting the doctor some eggs. Charles wandered off to his own room to wash, shave and put on a clean shirt. After about half an hour he returned. The doctor was in the same position as before, still snoring heavily. Charles and his mother went downstairs to have some breakfast. Some time later Mrs Lyddon returned upstairs to the still sleeping doctor. She tried to wake him, without success. She wetted a sponge, used it to wipe his face, but still without any noticeable response.

By nine o'clock they were becoming concerned. Charles remarked to his mother, 'This will not do, we must put him to bed with clean sheets,' and declared his intention of sending for Dr Evers. Mrs Lyddon called for Naylor and between them they made up the doctor's bed. While they were doing so, they could see Dr Lyddon through the open door, still apparently asleep.

When the bed was ready Naylor crossed over to the lumber-room and tried to rouse the sleeping man. He removed the bed-clothes, shook him gently and said, 'Come along doctor, you had better get into bed.' There was no kind of response. Naylor spent some time trying to wake him but without success.

While this had been going on Mrs Lyddon and Charles had been standing, watching. Now they told the boy to take the doctor to his own room and put him to bed. The two of them then just stood, making no attempt whatever to help, as the fifteen-year-old lad tried to move a grown man from the couch in one room to the bed in another. He was quite incapable of carrying him. With considerable difficulty he succeeded in getting him off the couch. He then dragged him, feet first, through into his own bedroom. The two adults continued to watch as Naylor tried, and failed completely, to lift the still sleeping man onto the bed.

It was only then that Mrs Lyddon offered any assistance. 'Wait a minute, Charles,' she said, 'and I will help you.' Her son still stood motionless while the young lad, helped by a woman of sixty-six, struggled to pick up the doctor and place him on the bed. They failed. The best that they were able to accomplish was to raise him into a half-sitting position leaning against the bed-post. And there they left him.

Charles and the boy descended the stairs together. 'You had better go and ask Dr Evers to come at once,' instructed Charles. 'Tell him that my brother is seriously ill.' Naylor did as he was told and returned, saying that he had seen Dr Evers who would be coming.

While Naylor had been away Charles Lyddon had been upstairs to see his brother who was clearly much worse, his breathing now barely perceptible. The boy was sent again to Dr Evers with the message that Dr Lyddon was dying. Dr Evers, not having come, Charles went outside to the stables. In the harness-room he found Francis Ford, his stable-man, together with a neighbour, Mr Woodruffe. He shouted to them that his brother was dying and called for someone to fetch Dr Boswell. On his return Naylor found Charles Lyddon in the hall, wringing his hands, while Mrs Lyddon stood on the landing, crying.

Dr Boswell arrived first and was met by Charles who led him upstairs where he discovered Dr Lyddon in a front bedroom. He was dressed, except for his coat and waistcoat. He lay face downwards on the floor, half under the bed. He had been dead for about an hour. Dr Evers now arrived on the scene and the two doctors examined the body together, while Charles watched. After a few minutes, he said to Dr Boswell:

'You have been attending my brother and must know what he died of.'

To this the doctor replied, 'I do not know what he died of and I shall certainly give no certificate.'

The three men then went downstairs together. As they did so Charles remarked, 'I suppose neither of you will give me a certificate, so I must send for the police.'

Both doctors nodded their agreement to this proposed course of action.

As was usual in the Lyddon household, Naylor was sent to the police station with a message for Inspector Fowle. The inspector not being immediately available, it was the appropriately named Police-Sergeant Frederick Sargent who returned with the boy to 12 West Street. The time was now 10.50 a.m.

It did not take long for P.S. Sargent to make his presence felt. Having asked to see the body of Dr Lyddon, he was led upstairs by Charles. The body lay stretched out on the floor beside the bed. There was a wet mark on the right cheek, the face wore a bluish tinge and the right cheekbone was discoloured.

'Where did your brother sleep last night?' asked the sergeant.

'In there,' said Charles, pointing to the lumber-room.

'Did he always sleep there?'

'No. He was ill last night and wanted to sleep there.'

The policeman went into the lumber-room where he found the blind still down. There was a dressing-table, a chest of drawers, three chairs, a few baskets, pieces of an organ and various other odds and ends. On the floor were items of clothing and bedding. Lying on a clothes-box close to the pillow was an 8oz medicine bottle. It lay flat, was tightly corked and contained a small quantity of a colourless liquid.

While the police officer was looking around, Charles had been watching from just inside the room. The sergeant showed him the bottle and asked,

'Can you account for this bottle being here?'

'Let me look at it,' said Charles.

The sergeant handed the medicine bottle to Charles who examined it closely.

'This settles the matter. I want you to take charge of this bottle,' remarked Charles, handing it back.

'I intend to,' replied the sergeant.

'I am glad you found this, as people might say I poisoned him,' commented Charles. Then he turned, leaned on the door-post and said,

'Oh, my poor brother. I only brought him back from Herne Bay yesterday and to think it has come to this.'

P.S. Sargent issued strict instructions that everything in the bedroom and lumber-room was to remain completely untouched until the inspector arrived. He then asked to see where the drugs were kept. Charles led him downstairs and into the surgery where he pointed to a row of bottles lying on a couch. The policeman examined them carefully until he found one that exactly matched that which he had found upstairs.

'How much of this do you have in at one time?' he asked.

'We had three bottles of the last lot,' he was told.

'Here are two of them, can you tell me what has become of the other one?'

'I don't know. I will ask the boy.'

'Can you say how much was in this bottle yesterday?'

'I could not say, but I should think enough to kill a dozen men.' At this point Charles Naylor, who had been called by Lyddon, entered the surgery. The sergeant showed him the bottle.

'Did you see the doctor with a bottle like this yesterday?' he asked.

'No,' replied Naylor after a quick look.

'Did he have a bottle like this when he went into the little-room?'

'No, or I should have seen.'

'Did you help him into the little-room?'

'Yes. He seemed to be ill. He took his coat off the bed, put it over his arm, but I did not see any bottle.'

The post-mortem showed the body to have bruises on the shoulder and on both sides of the trunk. Death had quite clearly been caused by morphia poisoning. The amount of morphia found in the body indicated a large and fatal dose, at least a quarter of a bottle. Death would have occurred within a few hours. It was also found that there was no whisky in the stomach, but more liquid than would have been expected in the stomach of someone who had had nothing to drink after midnight. If medical assistance had been requested at 7.30 a.m. his life could probably have been saved.

The coroner's inquest was held in Faversham Guildhall, in its room above the ancient market place, and lasted several days. A largish crowd stood outside throughout the hearings and made its own opinions quite clear by groaning loudly whenever Charles Lyddon put in an appearance. He submitted to the court a long and detailed account of events leading up to the death of his half-brother. In this account he claimed that, between midnight and 7.30 the next morning, no one entered the lumber-room. He said that the only key remained in his possession all night. Mrs Lyddon was declared to be too upset by her stepson's death to be able to give evidence. This was very unfortunate because various local witnesses claimed that they had been told by Mrs Lyddon that she had entered the little-room that night.

One such witness was Sarah Wise of Abbey Street who had helped Mrs Lyddon lay out the body. She claimed to have been told, by Mrs Lyddon, that she went three times to the little-room to see how the doctor was. She had said that she obtained the key from her son and had called him into the room to see the sleeping man, because she had been concerned about him.

At the end of the evidence the coroner's jury was told that it could come to one of three possible verdicts: suicide, misadventure or murder. After due consideration they declared, 'We believe that morphia was feloniously administered to the deceased by Charles Lyddon.'

The coroner called forward Mr Lyddon:

'It is my duty to commit you to take your trial at the next assize to be held at Maidstone upon the inquisition now found against you.'

The trial of Charles Lyddon did not, in fact, take place at Maidstone. Defence counsel objected on the grounds that he did not have enough time in which to prepare his case for the next assize; having to wait for the following assize would mean keeping the defendant under detention for too long a time. This was a very clever argument. There can be little doubt that counsel wanted his client tried outside the county of Kent where there was a great deal of feeling against him. His argument, however, was on purely administrative grounds.

In the eventual trial at the Old Bailey, before Mr Justice Hawkins, the evidence made familiar by the inquest and magisterial hearings was once more repeated. The prosecution made much of the morphia bottle which had so mysteriously appeared in the lumber-room between the removal of Dr Lyddon by Charles Naylor and the arrival of P.S. Sargent.

The defence argued that Dr Lyddon could have carried it into the little-room in his coat pocket and that it was overlooked by Naylor, the room being in darkness with the blinds down.

The two counsel finally rose to sum-up their respective cases. Firstly, Mr Murphy for the prosecution:

Although the assignment has been described as a family arrange-ment, which was satisfactory to everyone, it is difficult to know how it could have been satisfactory to the deceased as it placed everything at the disposal of the prisoner.

With regard to the fluid found in the deceased's stomach after death it must be pointed out that no water-bottle was found in the room which the deceased could have drunk from.

According to the prisoner's evidence he saw the deceased next morning breathing heavily and, although he knew that the deceased was in the habit of taking morphia, he left him there and did not call in medical assistance. Why was that? If medical assistance had been called in, the deceased's life would probably have been saved.

The conduct of the prisoner in leaving Naylor to move the deceased from the room without rendering him any assistance can hardly be realized.

Was the bottle, which was found in the room, there at half past seven in the morning when the prisoner went in?

Must not the prisoner have thought his brother was ill from morphia? The fluid found in the stomach of the deceased was quite inconsistent with a normal state of things, even in the case of a morphia taker. There was no trace of milk, stout or whisky in the stomach. The only way the fluid could be accounted for was by the deceased having taken some drink after he went to the room. How did the deceased get it? There was no water-bottle in the room. The inference was that someone went into the room. Who was that person? The prisoner alone kept the key and he must have been the person who went into the room if anyone did.

Mr Dickens, QC, for the defence, said that he had never risen to address a jury with less anxiety and more complete confidence, because the more the evidence was examined and probed the more completely did it appear how absolutely the charge had broken down. In a lengthy speech he made much of the fact that the two brothers lived on affectionate terms without, of course, mentioning that this only applied when they were both sober, which was not very often. He, quite rightly, placed great emphasis on the purely circumstantial nature of the evidence, casting doubts on all of it.

The deceased was a confirmed drug-taker and knew that the prisoner objected to his taking drugs. On the evening of 24 November the deceased had taken a dose of morphia and then put the bottle in his coat pocket. The craving would come on him again and, unless he took the bottle with him, he would not be able to satisfy it.

There can be little doubt that what really decided the minds of the jury was the summing-up of the case by Mr Justice Hawkins. He made his own opinion quite clear:

The prosecution in every case has the duty cast upon it of establishing the case by evidence which, in the judgement of the jury, is reliable. If the evidence left a reasonable doubt, then it is their duty to the prisoner, to their consciences and to the public to return an adverse verdict, unless the prosecution established the case by evidence which left no reasonable doubt.

Is it shown on the part of the prosecution that the deceased did not take the morphia with him into the bedroom? There is no evidence that it was not in the deceased's pocket. I cannot see why, if the prisoner wished to administer poison to the deceased, he should have put him in that room as it could have been done quite easily in the deceased's own bedroom.

After a summing-up like that, the jury took only two minutes to declare their verdict of 'Not Guilty'.

It has to be agreed that the judge and jury were quite correct in their decision to find Charles Lyddon not guilty on the evidence presented at the trial. But was he really not guilty?

It is greatly to be regretted that, while Charles Lyddon and Naylor gave their own accounts of the events of that night, the third member of that curious household did not. Mrs Lyddon avoided giving evidence at the inquest by claiming to be too upset. She could not be forced to give evidence against her son at his trial. But why did she stay silent? The significant thing about her behaviour at her son's trial is that, like the dog that didn't bark in the night, she did nothing. She could not be called by the prosecution, but she could have given evidence for the defence. She could have gone into the witness-box and confirmed everything that her son had said about events on that fateful night. Yet, she did not. She did and said nothing.

We know that in the immediate aftermath of her stepson's death she told several local people that she had entered the lumber-room several times between midnight and 7.30 a.m. The people who claimed to have been told this were of good character, with no reason whatever for lying about it. It is therefore highly likely that she did indeed go into that room. Since Charles Lyddon had the keys, he must have known about it, must have been party to it. Why then the secrecy? Why not say, 'Yes, we looked in several times during the night to see if he was all right.' What had those two people got to hide? It does not follow, of course, that because they went into the room, that they murdered him. But their denials are certainly curious.

The argument of the judge that, if Charles wished to murder his brother, there was no need to put him in the lumber-room, is easily refuted. If murder really was being planned Dr Lyddon and Naylor had to be parted. You cannot safely poison someone with a bright fifteen-year-old watching your every move. It is also noticeable that Charles, having placed the doctor in the lumber-room, also moved Naylor from his usual bedroom. Anyone planning to enter the lumber-room would have to cross the room normally occupied by both the doctor and Naylor. Charles ensured that it would be empty.

That Charles wanted the doctor dead is almost certain. How else to explain his behaviour, not only on the night that he died but when he had pneumonia two months earlier? Here we have a man with medical training, in the same house as someone suffering from severe pneumonia. What does he do? He totally neglects the patient and only brings in expert medical help when forced to do so by the interfering Dr Hill.

When, on that final morning, he finds his half-brother obviously so seriously ill that he cannot be woken, what does he do? He has him dragged about the house like a sack of potatoes and delays calling for help for two hours, until the patient is nearly dead.

If Charles Lyddon did not deliberately murder his half-brother he certainly avoided any action which might have prevented him from dying.

THE THIRD
COMPARTMENT

THE THIRD COMPARTMENT

O
n the coast of Northumberland, midway between Newcastle and the Scottish border, lies the small town of
Alnmouth. In common with many of the towns and villages
of England it has had a chequered history. Originating as the port for
Alnwick and sharing its long association with Harry Hotspur and
other colourful members of the Percy family, its fortunes have waxed
and waned with the varied levels of peace and prosperity of the
border area. After a long period of decline it became, in the
eighteenth century, a busy port, only to sink once more into obscurity
when the Aln river changed its course and effectively destroyed the
town's harbour. The coming of the railway, however, once more
brought the little town to life as a favourite seaside destination for the
prosperous middle classes of Newcastle.

By the end of the nineteenth century it had again become, in its
own quiet way, a small but prosperous community. Its railway
station, as with many similar places, is situated some distance from
the town, giving it a rather sleepy air, broken only by the occasional
Scottish express thundering through.

Shortly after midday on 18 March 1910, the 10.27 train from
Newcastle trundled slowly into Alnmouth station. It stopped amidst
a long hiss of steam, with that air of quiet satisfaction that only a
steam engine can give, like a man settling into a favourite armchair
after a long walk.

The foreman porter at Alnmouth, Thomas Charlton, raised a
hand in greeting to the engine-driver, now leaning on the side of his
cab. After watching the handful of passengers descend from the train,

Charlton began to stroll along the platform checking each compartment in turn. The train terminated its journey at Alnmouth and it was one of his responsibilities to ensure that it was clean and empty.

The first carriage comprised a luggage section, which he passed first, and then three third-class compartments. The first compartment was a smoker and was empty. The remaining two were non-smokers, the first of which was also empty and tidy. Charlton then approached the third compartment. Glancing in at the window he saw something on the seat nearest the engine. It looked wet. He opened the door, looking in as he did so. There was blood on the seat. As he opened the door wider he saw three streams of blood stretching across the floor.

Beneath the seat facing the engine was the body of a man. He lay on his stomach with his head under the seat. From his head trickled the three streams of blood. Lying amongst the blood were a pair of gold-rimmed spectacles, broken into two separate pieces, and a hard felt hat.

Charlton shouted for the guard who was still at the other end of the train attending to his parcels. Obviously nothing within the carriage could be touched until the police arrived, but something had to be done about the train. It was blocking the line and an express was due. The train was therefore shunted out of the station and brought back into another platform; this meant that the compartment could now be entered from the other side.

By now the local police had arrived upon the scene. There had never been much doubt that it was a case of murder. Men do not have accidents which leave them squeezed under the seats of railway carriages. The body was carefully pulled out from its hiding place. The man had quite obviously been shot several times. A spent bullet lay on the floor. He was about 5' 4" tall, slightly built and had a moustache.

The identity of the victim did not take long to establish. The police found him to be John Innes Nisbet of 180 Heaton Road, Newcastle, a book-keeper and cashier employed by the Stobswood Colliery Co. Once the police had contacted his employers the motive for the crime became obvious. At the time of his death he had been carrying the colliery wages; needless to say, the leather bag containing them had vanished.

It was learned from his employers that part of his duties with the colliery involved payment of wages. On alternate Fridays he was provided with a company cheque. This he presented to the bank and then took the proceeds, by train, to the colliery where he distributed them to the company employees. During the whole of the time of his visit to the bank and the subsequent train journey he was entirely unaccompanied. He was an easy target for anyone ruthless or desperate enough, especially as he carried out the process at precisely the same time every pay-day. In this he really had no choice. The nearest station to the colliery was Widdrington and should he fail to catch the 10.27 there was no other stopping train until 1.30 p.m.

On the morning of his death everything had gone exactly according to the long-established routine. Having been supplied with the necessary cheque by his employers he had gone to the Collingwood Street branch of Lloyds Bank. In return for the cheque he had been given cash to the value of £370-9s-7d. Some idea of the present-day value of that amount can be obtained from the fact that Nisbet's own salary was £2-15s a week. It was, therefore, the equivalent of about two-and-a-half years' salary for him.

The cash was given to Nisbet in the form of 231 sovereigns, 206 half-sovereigns, £35-9s in silver and £1-0s-7d in copper. The gold had been contained in three canvas bags, the silver in paper bags and the copper in a small brown-paper parcel. The whole amount had then been placed in a leather bag with a strong lock attached, the key for which Nisbet had tucked away for safety in an inside pocket. The leather bag bore the inscription 'No. 1 Lambton & Co. Newcastle', this being the name of a local bank recently taken over by Lloyds. After leaving the bank Nisbet made his way to Central Station where he purchased a ticket to Widdrington. He was well in time to catch the 10.27 train from platform 5.

An hour and a half later his body had been found. The post-mortem revealed that he had been shot in the head no less than five times. Four of the bullets were recovered, one from the carriage floor and three from his head. There were two distinct types of bullet: two each of nickel coated .25 and plain lead .32. The two types could not possibly be fired from the same gun. One of the bullets had hit him in the side of the head, at close range, while he was in an upright position, presumably seated. The remaining four were fired into his head as he lay on the floor. Ruthless and cold-blooded.

In their search for the killer or killers, the first obvious task for the investigating police officers was to identify and trace as many of the other passengers on the train as possible. This proved to be a great deal easier than might have been imagined.

The 10.27 train from Newcastle to Alnmouth was no Orient

Express; there was little romance about either its progress or the places that it served. It took ninety-nine minutes to travel thirty-four miles and the area travelled was that of small mining villages and sparsely populated farming country. Only the small but ancient town of Morpeth would be likely to appeal to even the most eager tourist and there were not many of those in March 1910. With its tall-chimneyed steam engine and elderly coaches it would, today, be an attraction in itself, but not then. Then it was a workaday train for workaday travel.

Many of its passengers were regulars, local people making the short journeys necessary for everyday life. Travel to and from work or the shops. Visits to relatives. All the normal humdrum movements of ordinary life that, in the age before the motor-car, were only made possible by such trains as the 10.27.

This local character of the train meant that the police had little of the difficulty in identifying passengers that they would have had had the crime taken place on one of the long-distance expresses which comprised most of the rail traffic on the route north of Newcastle. Many of the travellers were regulars and knew one another, at least by sight. It followed that, within a few days of the crime, the police were already beginning to get a reasonably clear picture of the movements of passengers on and off the train.

It had not been a long train, just an engine and four small coaches. As has already been explained, the first coach was a mixture of luggage-van and third-class compartments. The second coach had first-class compartments in the middle with third-class at each end. The third carriage was entirely third-class. The last coach was identical to the first and it was here that the guard travelled. When the train had stood beneath the vast roof of Newcastle Central Station there had been two additional carriages on the same line, but these were not part of the train and were not connected to it.

Two of the first passengers to come forward with information were especially useful to the police. They were John William Spink and Percival Harding Hall, both Newcastle men. Like Nisbet they were cashiers carrying colliery wages, in their case for the Northerton Coal Co. They, too, were regulars on the train, performing the same fortnightly task. Since they were on the same errand at the same time as Nisbet, they were very used to seeing him. Both men were aware that Nisbet was the cashier for the Stobswood Colliery.

On the day of the murder Hall and Spink travelled in the second compartment of the first carriage. After they joined the train at

Newcastle station, Hall stood with his head out of the window idly watching the bustle of activity on the platform. Passengers and station staff moving to and fro. The banging of doors. The nearby engine simmering quietly, waiting for the moment to exert itself. Shortly before the train was due to leave, he saw Nisbet come along the platform and climb aboard, into the compartment next to their own, the third compartment. There was another man with him.

The journey was completely uneventful. When Hall and Spink alighted from the train at Stannington, they had to wait on the platform for the train to leave before they could cross the line. The train slowly chuffed out of the little station. As it drew past them, so the two men saw Nisbet in his compartment. He was sitting facing the engine in the seat furthest from the platform. Hall nodded a greeting to him. There was a second man in the compartment, sitting opposite Nisbet, with his back to the engine in the seat furthest from the platform.

Other witnesses also came forward for this early part of the fatal journey.

Charles Raven, a commercial traveller of King John Terrace, Heaton, was particularly useful. He had known Nisbet for five or six years. On the morning in question, he had been standing close to the entrance of platform 4 at Newcastle Central. This was at the point where passengers for the Tyneside service separated from those bound for other destinations. He saw Nisbet walking with another man. They came from the direction of the third-class refreshment-room and passed behind a cigar-kiosk to platform 5. The man with Nisbet he knew, though only by sight, as John Dickman.

Quite soon this valuable piece of evidence was confirmed by another passenger on the 10.27, Wilson Hepple, an artist from Acklington. He had known John Dickman for twenty years. He told the police how, when the train came alongside the platform at Newcastle, he selected a compartment near the rear of the train. This compartment could easily be identified as, within it, was a picture of Brancepath Castle. This was soon discovered to be the third compartment of the third coach. Having found a suitable compartment, he mounted the carriage and deposited his parcels on the luggage-rack. As, however, there was still some time before the train was due to depart, he alighted once more and strolled on the platform, enjoying the atmosphere of a busy station. He did not move far from his compartment, not wanting to leave his parcels unguarded; about six paces in one direction, then turning and walking six paces back again.

While he was thus engaged, he saw two men, one of whom was certainly Dickman, walking together towards the front of the train, apparently in conversation. One of them reached out and took hold of a carriage door-handle, but at that moment Mr Hepple reached the limit of his walk, turned round and walked back to his own compartment. By now it was close to departure time and he therefore climbed into the train and took his seat. He did not see the two men get into the train. Judging by the description that he had read in the newspapers, he now believed that the man with Dickman could well have been the murdered Nisbet.

Mrs Cicely Nisbet, the murdered man's wife, was in the habit, when her husband caught the 10.27, of meeting it at Heaton Station, close to their home. On 18 March she went as usual to the station and, for the short time that the train stopped there, she saw and spoke to her husband. Having just come from the bank he was able to give her some housekeeping money for the weekend shopping. While they were talking she could see that there was another man in the compartment but, as he was sitting in the shadow of a nearby tunnel, she could only see his profile.

The picture for the early stages of the train journey was now fairly clear. According to Hall and Spink, Nisbet was alive and well when the train left Stannington. When, then, did the murder occur? The likely answer came from evidence given by a plate-layer, John Grant. The train's next stop after Stannington was Morpeth. This being the only town between Newcastle and its eventual destination a number of passengers left it at this point. But it was here that Grant joined it. As the train came slowly to a halt, he began to walk along it, starting at the engine. Like many railwaymen, he had the habit of looking into each compartment as he passed by it. The third compartment was empty. He walked a little further and climbed into the first compartment of the second carriage. It was now a quarter past eleven.

The staff at the other small stations beyond Morpeth were questioned and gave their own accounts of passenger movements.

George Harker, the station-master at Pegswood, saw two passengers leave the train, a woman with a little girl.

At the next station, Longhirst, the station-master, George Yeoman, saw three people get out, John Grant and a man and woman who had joined the train at Morpeth. A porter, John Croker, at the same station, observed passengers in the first compartment, but none in the third.

The next station along the line was Widdrington, Nisbet's

intended destination. The station-master there, John Yeoman, had been asked to look out for someone. He looked through the whole length of the train, without success. He also failed to see Nisbet who was, of course, a regular passenger at the small station.

At the next stop, Chevington, Andrew Bruce left the train. He was a carriage inspector who travelled in the first compartment of the first coach which he shared with another man. He confirmed that, when the train stopped at Stannington, two men left the compartment next to his, one of them nodding to someone in the third compartment.

There was nothing more of consequence to report until the train arrived at Alnmouth and the discovery of the body beneath the seat.

By Monday, 21 March, three days after the crime, many passengers of the 10.27 had come forward and made statements following the massive local press coverage. One man who was known to have been on the train, however, had not come forward. That man was John Alexander Dickman.

During the course of that Monday evening Detective-Inspector Tait went to 1 Lily Avenue, Jesmond, where Dickman lived with his wife and daughter. When the inspector reached the house his first thought was that he must have come to the wrong address. His discreet enquiries about Dickman had led him to believe that the man was short of money but the house gave a very different impression indeed. It was the home of a prosperous man.

It was therefore with some caution that he knocked at the door. The man who responded to his call proved, however, to be the John Dickman that he wished to question. Having gained admittance to the house the detective told Dickman that he had been informed that Dickman had been seen in the company of Nisbet on the morning of the murder. Dickman replied that the policeman's information was not strictly correct.

> I knew Nisbet for many years. I saw him that morning. I booked at the ticket window after him and went by the same train, but I did not see him after the train left. I would have told the police if I had thought it would have done any good.

He was then taken to the police station where he made a voluntary statement:

> On Friday morning last, I went to the Central Station and took a return ticket for Stannington. Nisbet, whom I knew, was at the ticket-office before me and had left the ticket-hall before I got mine. I went to the bookstall and got a paper, the *Manchester*

Sporting Chronicle. I then went to the refreshment-room and had a pie and a glass of ale. I then went to the platform and took my seat in a third-class carriage near the rear. The train passed Stannington without my noticing it and I got out at Morpeth and handed my ticket with the excess $2\frac{1}{2}$d to the collector.

I left Morpeth to walk to Stannington by the main road. I took ill of diarrhoea on the way and had to return to Morpeth to get the 1.12 p.m. train, but missed it. I had to get the 1.40. While at Morpeth, after missing the 1.12, I came out of the station on the east side and turned down towards the town. I met a man named Elliot and spoke to him. I did not get into the town, but turned and went back to the station.

In view of the evidence already given by the other travellers on the train and the obvious discrepancies between their accounts and that given by John Dickman, he was shortly afterwards formally charged with the murder of John Nisbet. When cautioned by Superintendant Weddell he said, 'I do not understand the proceedings, it is absurd for me to deny the charge because it is absurd to make it. I only say that I absolutely deny it.'

At the time of his arrest Dickman had in his possession £17-9s-11d, including £15 in gold, in a bag marked 'No. 1 Lambton & Co. Newcastle'. Enquiries revealed that only a few days before the murder he had been short of money. Searching his house the police found pawn-tickets relating to a pair of field-glasses.

Extensive enquiries revealed that, on 15 October 1909, he had gone to the office of a money-lender, Samuel Cohen, where he had asked for the loan of £20. He said that he only needed it for three months. Upon being told that the interest rate would be £1 a month, he declared indignantly that that was much too high, but that he would think about it. He returned later, accepted the terms and was lent £20. The interest was paid but three months later, when the repayment of the principal became due, he asked for and was granted an additional three months, plus of course another £3 in interest.

Two bank pass-books were found, one for the National Provincial Bank and one for Lambton's Bank. There was no money in either of them, both having been closed during the previous December.

While Dickman had been undergoing determined police questioning the funeral of the murdered man took place. The procession from his home in Heaton to his final resting-place in Jesmond cemetery was watched by crowds of people. They lined the Newcastle streets, standing motionless, heads bowed in respect. The men with their hats in their hands, the women with handkerchiefs to their eyes as the hearse slowly passed. Amongst the mourners were a partner in the firm which owned Stobswood Colliery and the colliery manager. There were also representatives of the colliery workmen.

The great wave of emotion put additional pressure on the police to obtain a conviction and made any prospect of a genuinely fair trial anywhere on Tyneside increasingly unlikely.

An identity parade was now held in the police station. Spink and Hall were both invited to identify the man that they had seen in Nesbit's compartment on the 10.27. Upon their arrival at the police station the two men were invited by a constable to look through an internal window at Dickman who was waiting with a uniformed policeman for the identity parade. Luckily, as the window was partly frosted, they could not see him clearly. It was also suggested that they might care to look through a half-open door, again to see Dickman before the identity parade. They only saw his light-coloured coat.

In spite of these disgraceful attempts to influence their judgement the two cashiers retained their natural honesty. Spink was not prepared to admit to any recognition at all. Hall, after an inspection of the line of nine men, indicated Dickman and declared that 'he was like the man in the train', but was not prepared to swear to it. The police were unwise enough to pressure him in an attempt to get a more definite response. 'If I was assured that the murderer was in amongst those nine men, I would have no hesitation in picking the prisoner out,' was the furthest that Hall would go.

It would be interesting to know just how that identity parade was organized. Were the other eight men wearing similar clothes to Dickman? Or of similar age and height? It seems unlikely. Certainly Hall and Spink emerged from the incident with a great deal more credit than the police. The gross irregularities of police behaviour only emerged after the trial was over and the verdict had been given.

Mrs Cicely Nisbet was also faced with the identity parade but she, too, was unable to declare that any of the men was the one who was sharing her husband's compartment at Heaton Station. Later, after giving evidence at a magistrate's hearing, she fainted immediately upon leaving the witness-box. Several days later she came forward and declared that she had fainted because, as she rose to leave the court, she had seen Dickman from the same angle as the man in the train.

She was now absolutely certain that Dickman was the man that she had seen with her husband on the day of his death. Again it was not until after the trial that it emerged that she had known Dickman slightly, long before the murder.

The police had meanwhile been searching for the missing money and the murder weapons. They went to Dickman's house, dug up his garden, took his piano to pieces, searched the cistern and lifted his carpets. Entirely without success.

For his part, Dickman greatly extended his own account of his movements on 18 March. He claimed to have left home at ten o'clock that morning. He wore a suit, a black hat, a brown overcoat, brown gloves and black boots. He caught a tram from the end of his street to Northumberland Avenue and then walked down Grey Street and through High Bridge. Once on the train, in a compartment near the rear, he had settled down to study his newspaper. It was especially interesting that day because it was Grand National day and he was a keen betting man. Being so deeply engrossed in the paper he had completely missed his station, only becoming aware of it when the train swerved sharply to negotiate the tight bend on the approach to Morpeth. It had not concerned him too much because his intended destination was situated between Stannington and Morpeth so that he could easily approach it from either station.

It was his intention to visit a contractor, William Hogg, who was sinking a new shaft at Dovecot, some three-and-a-half miles from Morpeth or one-and-a-half miles from Stannington. On the way there he proposed to see a drift-mine which delivered coal on to the Newcastle road. This was midway between Stannington and Morpeth. He was interested in seeing the quantity of coal being produced.

In carrying out this programme it had been his original intention to go first to Dovecot and then to the drift, which was nearer to Morpeth. He would then continue his walk to Morpeth and return to Newcastle from there. Morpeth being a much larger place than Stannington, more trains stopped there. As a result of his failure to leave the train at Stannington, however, he now proposed to carry out these two errands in the reverse order.

After paying the 2½d excess fare to the ticket-collector at Morpeth he set out along the Newcastle road. When he reached a point approximately halfway between the two small settlements of Catch-burn and Clifton, he suddenly began to feel very bad. The reason for his discomfort was that he suffered from piles, a fact that he had omitted from his original statement out of embarrassment. Having left the road, he tried to relieve himself, without success. He then lay on the grass for about half an hour before, feeling somewhat better, he returned to Morpeth, hoping to catch the express.

Questioned as to his financial position, Dickman was able to explain to the police that a few years earlier he had been secretary to a colliery company at Morpeth. While in their employment he had been instrumental in organizing a takeover of that company at a very favourable price. For this service he had been paid about £400 in commission but, after the takeover, he had no longer been required by the company. Since then he had been making a living by betting on horses, both with his own money and as an adviser. This was by no means a case of speculating with small sums; he quite frequently bet substantial amounts – £10, £50, even £100. He was also occasionally paid useful sums in commission from bookmakers for diverting business in their direction. As for the recent sudden change in his financial position, it was in the very nature of betting that sometimes you were relatively well-off and at other times somewhat short.

When the police questioned the ticket-collector at Morpeth he confirmed Dickman's story. He had indeed presented a ticket valid only as far as Stannington and had paid 2½d excess fare which he had had ready in his hand when he approached the barrier. The railwayman declared that he saw no bag in Dickman's hand. He did have his overcoat over his arm, but the leather bag containing the colliery wages was far too big to be simply hidden under a coat.

William Hogg, the contractor at Dovecot, whom Dickman claimed he was going to see, was not even in the area on that day. He was, in point of fact, attending a business meeting in Newcastle. He did confirm that Dickman had been to see him at Dovecot some four or five times, always without prior appointment. The last occasion had been on the Friday two weeks before the murder. Mr Hogg was by no means sure why Dickman kept coming to visit him, he was doing no business with him.

Until now, apart from the £17 found in Dickman's pocket which may or may not have come from the stolen wages, no trace of either the money or the guns had been discovered. Then, on 9 June, Peter Spooner, the colliery manager at Barmoor East Colliery near Morpeth, set out to examine the air-shaft for the No. 1 seam. While carrying out this routine inspection he found, at the bottom of the air-shaft, a leather bag which bore the inscription 'No. 1 Lambton & Co. Newcastle'. The bottom of the bag had been slit open with a knife; of the original contents only a few coppers remained. A careful search of the shaft bottom produced copper coins to the value of 14s-8d. There were no traces of either more valuable coins or the murder weapon. Barmoor East Colliery was situated to the south-east of Morpeth, on the opposite side of the railway track to the Newcastle road.

During the month of July 1910 John Dickman was brought before Lord Coleridge at the Northumberland County Assizes held in the Moot Hall at Newcastle. This was not perhaps a sensible decision, there being a great deal of emotion in the Newcastle area about the case. There were claims both before and after the trial that Dickman could not possibly have a fair hearing in such a heady atmosphere and before a Newcastle jury.

In describing the trial, it has to be declared immediately that the prosecution case was quite remarkably thin. What evidence there was against Dickman was entirely circumstantial and much of that of very dubious value.

An attempt to produce hard, forensic evidence came in the form of statements from Dr R. Bolam, a professor from Durham University. He had been asked, by the police, to examine Dickman's clothing. He testified before the court that he had found traces of blood on the thumb of Dickman's left glove. Similar traces were also found in his left-hand trouser pocket. In both cases they were tiny spots of blood and were less than two weeks old.

This evidence appeared to be of great importance until, questioned by counsel, the professor was unable to say whether or not the blood was the murdered man's or indeed whether or not it was human blood! Dickman said that he had had a nose bleed.

The professor then went on to tell the court that he had also discovered a stain on the front of Dickman's coat which he said could have been caused by paraffin which may have been used to remove a blood-stain! Dickman said that he had got bicycle oil on it.

It is difficult to understand how anybody could have been expected to take such nonsense seriously. Similar 'evidence' could have been found on the clothing of half the population of Newcastle.

Virtually the only evidence against John Dickman was evidence of identity and much of that was almost as worthless as the forensic evidence.

Of the people on the train, Spink could not identify him at all and Hall could only say that he was similar to the man that he saw with Nesbit. Hardly enough to convict a man of murder.

Mrs Nesbit failed to pick him out at an identity parade, even one organized by the Newcastle police, but claimed to recognize him when she saw him in the dock at the magistrates' court. This, again, is not evidence that should be acceptable by any court. It is far too easy for a witness to say, 'Yes, that's the man,' when he is already standing in the dock.

The only evidence of any value presented to the court was that given by the two men, Hepple and Raven, who both saw him at Newcastle Central Station. If those two men were right – and there was no reason for disbelieving them – then Dickman was with Nisbet on the platform. There was no evidence whatever that they travelled together. If, when questioned, Dickman had said, 'Yes, I saw Nisbet that day, as a matter of fact we walked down the platform together, but we got into separate compartments because I wanted a smoke,' there would have been no real evidence against him at all. But he did not say that. He denied being with, or talking to, Nisbet that day. And that is what hanged him. For, in spite of the paucity of real evidence, Dickman was indeed found guilty and sentenced to death.

The immediate affect of Dickman's conviction was a nationwide cry of disbelief and indignation. A clamorous argument broke out not only in the north-east but throughout the country and even abroad. An argument that soon became so violent that both sides forgot all about Dickman sitting in the condemned cell and contented themselves with throwing insults at each other. This was reflected in the snowstorm of letters published in the Newcastle press.

Sir,
Dickman convicted! Who then is safe? No actual proof. Suspicion if you like. He should have had the benefit of the doubt. The evidence was not enough to hang a dog.
Horrified & Indignant, Yorkshire

Sir,
I venture to say that nine persons out of every ten are of the opinion that Dickman has been found guilty on evidence which besides being circumstantial is woefully insufficient.
Dunelmian

Sir,
If a person is to be hanged upon such flimsy evidence as that against Dickman – and the whole of it circumstantial, mark you – then no one, however innocent, will stand any chance should the police prefer a charge of murder.
Medio Tutissimus Ibis

... the same methods could make some sort of a case out against any passenger known to have travelled on that train, who could not produce chance passengers as witnesses or against any man spoken to by Nisbet that morning.

John Lindsey

As another earnest student of the train murder I, with the majority of others, consider the verdict passed on Dickman a very proper and fit one, and too good for such an undoubted scoundrel. Evidently we have a lot of unbalanced, morbid sentimentalists amongst us. Anyone with a grain of common-sense would certainly agree that no other verdict was possible.

Recte et Suaviter

Sir,

I would be glad if you would extend to me the courtesy of your columns to allow me to express my amazement at the jury's verdict in the train murder case. As one who was present throughout the trial, it struck me that it would have been as easy for the police, had they turned their ingenuity in that direction, to have manufactured quite as good a case against any other person who had travelled by the 10.27 train as against Dickman.

Citizen

The verdict in the case and the sentence are simply out of all proportion to the evidence.

One Just Man

I have read the letters of 'Citizen', 'Dunelmian' and John Lindsey and I confess I have never read such humbug . . . No judge could have been fairer. His long drawn-out summary was a legal masterpiece, showing clearly that Dickman had not been truthful in the witness-box.

Hexhamonian

What a gross act of injustice to condemn this man to death on the evidence that has been given. It is a crime evidently to be hard up and pawn a few of one's belongings.

A Lover of Justice

. . . to the casual reader, he seems to have done on the day of the murder everything that a guilty man would have avoided doing. If Dickman is guilty, what did he do with the pistols and the money? There is not a scrap of evidence to connect him with the possession of either.

A. Cameron

What a strange people we are. No matter how atrocious a crime is in its detail, or how cold-blooded and callous in its execution, we always find people who are not only ready to sympathize with the prisoner, but even to sing a paeon of praise in his favour. One of your correspondents exclaimed with a dramatic air, 'Dickman convicted, who is safe?' Let me ask him another and more important one, viz, fellows like Dickman not convicted, who then indeed is safe?

Notanda

Dickman is the only person on whom any suspicion rests, mark you, I say suspicion, but we as Englishmen, who like to see fair-play, and who won't hit a man when he is down, surely cannot allow a life to be taken on suspicion. No one can safely say that Dickman murdered Nisbet.

Emanus

I think if some of your correspondents in the Dickman case had thought the matter over carefully and weighed it up thoroughly we would not have had so many effusions of silly, sloppy, sentiment.

J.

I am the only brother of the condemned man and am truly sorry for him in his position, and also grieved to think that he should so far have lost his self-control necessary to restrain him in committing such a crime. But I cannot allow my grief to outweigh my conscience as to right and wrong. Can anyone after reviewing his own evidence, unless they look through smoked glass, conscientiously say he is an innocent man?

Wm. Dickman

Is it not perfectly amazing and indeed pitiful that no matter how atrocious a crime may be committed in this country, there is always a large number of people ready to sympathize with the murderer?

Let Justice be Done

An appeal was made on behalf of John Dickman and petitions raised not only in the north-east but in Glasgow, Dundee, Brighton, Chatham and Southend. Amongst its many distinguished signatories was Sir R.D. Yelverton, former Chief Justice of the Bahamas. But it was all to no avail. The Court of Appeal could see no reason for questioning the verdict of the Newcastle jury and, despite the nationwide clamour, John Dickman was duly hanged.

But did he do it? The police clearly thought so. They believed that it was a carefully premeditated crime. They believed that Dickman had travelled time and time again on that same train, on alternate Fridays, watching Nisbet's habits and using William Hogg as an excuse for these otherwise unnecessary journeys. Certainly Mr Hogg knew of no reason why Dickman made frequent visits to see him without appointment.

On the day of the murder Dickman organized a meeting with Nisbet, perhaps in the station booking-hall, walked on to the platform with him and they joined the train together without Nisbet having any reason for suspicion. Dickman deliberately sat in the darkest, least conspicuous corner of the compartment.

He clearly could not risk committing the murder until after Stannington, because Hall and Spink might have heard the shots. In any case they would expect to see Nisbet in the compartment when they left the train.

Once the compartment next door was safely empty it was a simple matter to stand up, perhaps ostensibly to attend to a coat on the rack. By the time the relaxed, unsuspecting Nisbet had realized what was happening it was too late.

The money-bag and possibly the guns were then thrown out of the window while the train was negotiating the long sharp curve before Morpeth. Dickman left the train perfectly casually, made his way back towards Stannington and retrieved the money and guns which he then hid, keeping only sufficient cash for his immediate needs.

All this is perfectly reasonable and logical. It may well have happened like that. But was it proved? The answer has to be that it was not. On balance, at the trial of John Dickman, justice was probably done, whether it was *seen* to be done is another question. Certainly the trial should never have been held at Newcastle with so much pressure put upon local jurymen to convict.

The violent death of John Nisbet also resulted in another case for the courts, this time for the civil court and one which, eventually, certainly did reach the correct conclusion.

Following the sudden death of her husband Mrs Nisbet applied for compensation from his employers, the Stobswood Colliery Co., under the recently enacted Workmen's Compensation Act. The colliery no doubt considered that they had already lost more than enough in the £370 stolen wages and that they had done their duty to their former employee by attending his funeral and sending a wreath. To their shame they disputed the claim.

Their argument was that the Act only awarded compensation when a workman was killed in an accident while at work. Nisbet clearly did not die in an accident, he was murdered, and therefore his widow could not possibly be entitled to any compensation from her husband's employers.

The case was considered by the Court of Appeal. The Master of the Rolls referred to a previous case in which a gamekeeper, while on duty, had been murdered by poachers. In that case the presiding judge had ruled that the death of the gamekeeper was covered by the Act since the man's death arose directly out of his employment. This quite obviously also applied to Nisbet. His widow, therefore, received £300 compensation, about two years' salary.

A PENSION FOR
LIFE

A PENSION FOR
LIFE

At the tail end of 1909 Frederick Henry Seddon had every reason to be content with his position in life. From modest origins – his father described himself as a 'watch finisher' – he had by care and diligence established a pleasant and comfortable existence. He had a good job, an attractive wife, delightful children, a large house, was well fed and clothed and had more than adequate financial reserves. Most of his fellow men during that last year of Edward's reign would have regarded his position as enviable. And yet, he was not content, he could never know contentment, because he had an obsession, an obsession that dominated his life and was soon to destroy him – a deep and abiding passion for money.

It is a curious fact that the people who become totally obsessed with money are not the poor. They would at least have an excuse for it, but are kept by bare necessity close to the reality of things. To them money is as it should be, simply a means of exchange. You cannot eat money or wear it on your back, but you can use it to obtain food and clothing. In itself it is worthless, there is really little point in piling it up. Money is only really important when you have not got any.

Frederick Seddon was by no means short of money but he was an old-fashioned miser. His great pleasure in life was counting his money; the sheer physical pleasure of counting gold sovereigns, of building them into little piles and finding that he had more than he had had the previous month. He also collected properties, strictly for investment of course, and equally enjoyed calculating their values and the rents that could be squeezed out of them.

He and his family lived in a large house but were cramped into

145

only a small number of rooms, with partitions dividing them up, in an effort to make a profit out of his ownership of the building and further boost his stock of money. He collected money in the same way some men collect stamps or first editions.

He combined this passion for money with the more usual pretentiousness of the English lower middle class. He liked to feel that he was someone of importance, someone that other men looked up to as one of their betters. This would have been fine had he really been someone of importance, someone really worth looking up to. But the truth of the matter was that he was a nobody. Just an insurance salesman. Of no more, or less, importance than a million other citizens of the great city of London in which he lived.

Seddon resided, for he was far too grand to simply live anywhere, in Tollington Park, just north of the Seven Sisters Road and in close proximity to Finsbury Park, north London. Tollington Park is, despite its name, not a park at all but a fairly ordinary road. It is still today, in spite of the invasion of modern blocks of flats, remarkable for the ornateness of its Victorian architecture. In 1909 the snobbery must have been overwhelming.

Number 63, Seddon's home, was a large house, fourteen rooms behind its red-and-yellow brick facade. The basement could be reached by an outside flight of steps near the front door, in addition to internal stairs. It was here that Seddon had his office for which he charged his employers 5s a week. There was also a back kitchen. On the ground floor were two reception rooms. On the first floor the two bedrooms had each been divided by partitions to provide space for all of Seddon's family.

In addition to his wife, Margaret, there were five children, William aged seventeen, Maggie aged sixteen, Freddie fifteen, Ada eight and Lily who was not yet one year old. Also living with them were Seddon's elderly father and one servant, Mary Chater, who was grossly overworked and almost certainly disgracefully underpaid. All these nine people slept in discomfort in the two partitioned rooms on the first floor. This arrangement enabled Seddon to look for suitable tenants for the top, unoccupied floor of the house.

Seddon was employed by the London & Manchester Assurance Company as Superintendant of Canvassers for North London, a kind of local sales manager. He had worked for the company for almost twenty years and received average weekly earnings, including commission, of about £5-16s.

In addition to being paid 5s a week for using his home as an office, he was allowed 3s-9d for postage. His eldest son also worked for the company as an insurance agent, bringing in 14s a week.

In view of the picture already given of the character of Frederick Seddon it is not surprising to learn that his marriage was not entirely a happy one. He and his wife had indeed separated for a time. By November 1909 they were once more living together, however, and by raising a £300 mortgage he completed the purchase of 63 Tollington Park.

By the following July, having successfully squeezed his family into the lower part of the house, Seddon was ready to further augment his income. Through a local agency he offered to let the top floor for a rent of 12s a week. This comprised a bedroom at the front with a small kitchen alongside; at the rear was a second bedroom and a tiny box-room.

His new tenants moved in on 25 July. The most important of these newcomers was Eliza Mary Barrow, a forty-nine-year-old spinster who, for a number of years, had lived with a succession of relatives, never staying with any of them very long. She was by all accounts eccentric. She was dirty, always scruffily dressed, quick to take offence and generally difficult to live with. Without any apparent cause, she would sometimes go for a week or more refusing to speak to anyone, relying upon terse written notes to make clear her demands. She was also notoriously mean.

Immediately prior to moving into the Seddon household she had been living with her cousin, Frank Vanderahe, at 31 Evershot Road, just around the corner from Tollington Park. For some totally obscure reason she chose suddenly to adopt an attitude of sulking silence, thereby ensuring that everyone in the house was thoroughly miserable. The first indication that they received of her intention to leave them was when she placed a notice on the table at breakfast announcing her imminent departure. It is highly unlikely that their reaction was anything other than relief.

With her to the Seddon home came Ernest Grant, a nine-year-old orphaned nephew whom she had chosen to adopt and whom she rarely allowed out of her sight. There were also two other relatives, Mr and Mrs Robert Hook. Mr Hook worked as an engine-driver. It was intended, very optimistically, that Mrs Hook would teach Miss Barrow to cook, thereby making her less dependent upon 'ungrateful relatives'.

Miss Barrow was by no means poor, in fact she was rather well off. She owned £1600 in India Government Stock which brought her £52 a year in interest. She also held leases in a Camden Town public-house, the Bucks Head, together with a barber's shop next door to it. These properties, after allowing for ground rents, produced £120 a year net. She had about £200 in the Finsbury & City of London Bank and lastly, but by no means least, she had a cash-box. The box contained, in addition to a ring and a gold watch and chain, at least £200 in gold sovereigns.

Seddon, with his well-tuned nose, did not take very long to smell money. Once smelt, its odour became irresistible. He began to plot for its acquisition. Only fifteen days after their arrival he was successful in forcing Mr and Mrs Hook out of the house. On the Saturday evening Mr Hook had some shirts to collect from the laundry and, the weather being fine, he asked Miss Barrow if she would care to go for a walk. She seemed to find the idea attractive and they had a pleasant stroll together, sitting for a while in a local park. Miss Barrow was in an unusually friendly frame of mind and talked about the public-house that she owned.

The next afternoon, the warm weather continuing, Mr and Mrs Hook took young Ernie out for a walk as far as Barnet, getting back at about six. Shortly after their return, sixteen-year-old Maggie Seddon delivered a note to them from Miss Barrow in which she ordered them to leave the house at once. Mr Hook, naturally annoyed, returned it by the same means that it had come, but not before writing his reply on the back:

Miss Barrow,
As you are so impudent to send the letter to hand, I wish to inform you that I shall require return of my late mother's & sister's furniture & the expense of my moving here and away.

Soon afterwards, young Maggie once more came up the stairs saying that her father wished to see Mr Hook immediately. She went down again with a message that, if Mr Seddon wished to see Mr Hook, he should come upstairs himself, not keep sending his daughter. This message did indeed bring Seddon stamping up the stairs in what was quite obviously a foul mood, to be met at the top by an equally angry Hook.

'You want to see me?'

'I see you do not mean to take any notice of Miss Barrow's notice ordering you to leave.'

'No. Not at this time of night.'

'I give you twenty-four hours' notice to leave.'

'I will if I can and if I can't I will take forty-eight hours.'

'I do not know whether you know it or not, but Miss Barrow has put all her affairs in my hands.'

'Has she? Including her money?'

'No.'

'I will defy you and a regiment like you to get her money in your hands.'

'I don't want her money. I am just going to look after her interests.'

At half past one in the morning, Mr and Mrs Hook were woken by a most curious tapping noise on their bedroom door. Mr Hook called out:

'Who is that?'

'All right Hook,' came the reply from Mr Seddon, 'now you go out of here careful and quietly tomorrow.'

Curious to learn what their landlord had been up to in the middle of the night, Mr Hook climbed out of bed and crossed the room. Opening the door he discovered a note fastened to the outside:

'You and your wife have treated me so badly this day that I order you to leave at once.'

Although the note had Miss Barrow's name at the bottom it was not in her handwriting. Mr and Mrs Hook left the house the next day and never returned.

It was now 11 August and, with the Hooks safely out of the way, Seddon was able steadily to increase his influence over Miss Barrow. He had the great advantage in that he and the eccentric spinster loved the same thing, money. It enabled him fully to understand his opponent and exploit her natural weaknesses.

His first target was the £1600 nominal of India stock. It is always easy for anyone with even a rudimentary knowledge of investment to cast doubts, especially when he is dealing with someone with no knowledge at all of the subject, just a constant, nagging fear of losing her money. With his pose as a disinterested friend having a long professional experience in financial matters he was soon expressing concern about her having such a large sum of money invested with the Government of India. As a short-term investment it was, of course, perfectly safe and had provided a good yield in the past. But as a long-term investment? With knowing looks and an air of concern came references to riots in Calcutta or a late monsoon. Perhaps a fall in the price of tea or the level of world interest rates? By these means he was able to frighten the woman with the prospect of financial ruin.

Then came the master stroke. What she really ought to do was to safeguard her future income by exchanging her dangerously volatile India stock for an annuity. That way she could always be sure that her income was safe. And who was there who could organize such an annuity for her? Why, her friendly, disinterested financial adviser.

It might be imagined that, since Seddon was an employee of London & Manchester Assurance, he would place the business through the company in the normal way. But that was not the idea at all, he did not just want the commission, he wanted the capital.

Without taking any genuine independent advice, on 14 October Miss Barrow transferred ownership of the India stock to Seddon. In return, she received a verbal promise of £108 a year. Seddon then sold the stock for £1520, invested it in leases on fourteen tenement houses in the East End and was soon receiving £200 a year in rents. A very successful deal, especially for the financial adviser.

Having pulled off such a brilliantly successful coup, Seddon could hardly be expected to leave it at that. His mind began to turn towards Miss Barrow's property. A public-house and a barber's shop. What he could do with them!

But he took his time. He behaved like a skilled angler with a big fish and played it with infinite care. The annuity promised in return for the India stock was paid with scrupulous regularity and it was more than she had been receiving in dividends before. What wise advice! What a kind and knowledgeable friend! So different from grasping relatives!

But ownership of a public-house? In the past, of course, a very sound and sensible investment. But in the future? What about the Liberal government? What about that dangerous radical, Lloyd George? Talk of higher taxes on alcohol. Threats of shorter licencing hours. What would they do to the capital value of a public-house? Surely another annuity would be so much more sensible?

On 11 January 1911 Miss Barrow transferred the ownership of her property to Frederick Seddon in return for a second annuity. She was to receive £52 a year for life. On this occasion she was even given an agreement in writing. But Seddon was clearly becoming ever more greedy. While he was much more generous in giving out pieces of paper of dubious value, in terms of real cash the picture was very different. In this new deal he received property bringing in £120 a year and, in return, promised to pay the princely sum of £52 a year. Another successful investment.

With most of Miss Barrow's assets now safely in his own sticky hands and showing a useful profit Seddon was, for a little while, satisfied. But that was not a state of affairs that could be expected to last. During June 1911 Miss Barrow went to the office of the Finsbury & City of London Bank in Upper Street, Islington. She withdrew the whole of her investment there, £216, which she insisted on collecting in gold. With her on this little expedition went Mrs Seddon. The whole of that £216 promptly disappeared without trace.

But, by that summer of 1911, Frederick Seddon was becoming less and less satisfied with his financial arrangements with Miss Barrow. Having all her assets was fine, but this continuous payment to her of £3 a week was a serious drain upon his resources. And it was for life! She was only forty-nine. She could easily live another twenty years, perhaps even thirty years. £3 a week for thirty years. It didn't bear thinking about. And in any case, the lease of the Bucks Head was due to expire in sixteen years. He would then be paying money out and getting none in. On the other hand, she might die quite soon. And the annuities would die with her. That would be much more convenient. Would do wonders for his financial situation.

On 5 August, Miss Barrow travelled to Southend for a short holiday. Nine-year-old Ernie Grant naturally went with her, as did Mrs Seddon. They all returned together three days later, on the 8th.

Towards the end of that hot August sixteen-year-old Maggie Seddon was sent to a chemist's shop not far from her home. There she purchased a packet of six flypapers. The packet carried a very clear warning that they contained a dangerous poison, arsenic.

Just one week later Miss Barrow suddenly fell ill with sickness and diarrhoea. She was confined to bed and a local doctor, Dr Sworn, was consulted. He diagnosed epidemic diarrhoea, a common enough illness in the summer months at a time when hygiene was little understood. Dr Sworn prescribed suitable medicines and called to see his patient every day. For two more days her symptoms continued, in spite of the medicines; this state of affairs greatly puzzled the doctor who had always found them effective in similar cases. Then, however, she just as suddenly began to improve. The improvement continued each day that the doctor came to see her, until 11 September.

On that day, between six and seven in the evening, after the doctor had left and without having mentioned it to him, Miss Barrow made a will. It was not a lengthy document, the contents being remarkably straightforward, although written in carefully correct legal language. In it she appointed Frederick Seddon to be sole executor of all her personal belongings. Her money, furniture, clothing and jewellery were to be held in trust, by him, for her niece and nephew, Hilda and Ernest Grant, until they reached the age of twenty-one. At this point he was free to choose whether to distribute the property between them or to sell it for cash and divide the proceeds. The witnesses to the will were Seddon's wife and father.

Strange to relate, soon after making that will, Miss Barrow took a sudden turn for the worse. Only two days later, on 13 September when Dr Sworn called to see her again, expecting to find her now completely recovered, he discovered that she was obviously much worse. The doctor was quite unable to account for this state of affairs.

That same evening, Frederick Seddon attended a theatre, the Marlborough, apparently alone. He reached there shortly after 7.30 p.m. and had a protracted argument at the box-office over whether he had submitted a florin or a half-crown. His wife remained at home with her sister-in-law, Mrs Longley from Wolverhampton, who, together with her fourteen-year-old daughter, was staying with the Seddons.

With Frederick out of the house and the children all safely tucked up in bed, the two women settled down for a nice feminine chat. The boy, Ernest Grant, shared Miss Barrow's bed, as was invariably the custom. Miss Barrow insisted on the young lad sleeping in her bed even during her very unpleasant illness.

For a while the house was delightfully quiet, then the two women heard a great cry from the ill woman upstairs:

'I am dying.'

They rushed upstairs together. The woman in the bed complained of violent pains in the stomach and said that her feet were freezing cold. Acting on the advice of her sister-in-law, Margaret Seddon wrapped a petticoat around the woman's feet. They then prepared and applied hot flannels to her stomach. After doing their best to make her comfortable, they lowered the gas and returned down-stairs, with a new subject for conversation.

But they were not to be left in peace for long. Mr Seddon returned from the theatre to be told the details of the evening's alarm. Almost immediately the boy came downstairs with new complaints from Miss Barrow. Seddon and Mrs Longley proceeded upstairs together to investigate. Mrs Longley considered it unhealthy for a young boy to share a bed with a sick woman and said so in no uncertain fashion. Seddon told Miss Barrow that she really must go to sleep.

For a while everything was quiet. Mrs Longley retired to bed. Shortly afterwards Mr and Mrs Seddon also withdrew for the night.

But the peace was not to last. The Seddons were woken by young Ernie bearing a new message from Miss Barrow. Questioned, he told them that she was very restless, continually tossing and turning. Mrs

Seddon went to see for herself and found the situation wholly unchanged from her last visit. The boy was instructed to go and sleep in another room. Miss Barrow called him back. Seddon sent him away again.

The next time that the sick woman called out, Frederick said that he would go. They both went. Miss Barrow had fallen out of bed. She lay on the floor with the boy trying to help her up. Seddon lifted her back onto the bed and once more sent away the nine-year-old, telling him to go to sleep.

Miss Barrow now asked Margaret Seddon to stay with her and this she agreed to do, sitting on a chair close to the bed. After a while the sick woman seemed, at last, to go to sleep. Seddon, looking in and seeing Miss Barrow apparently sound asleep, suggested to his wife that she ought now to return to her own bed and get some sleep herself. This she declined to do.

'What is the good?' she said. 'She will only call me again.'

And so it continued for some hours – Miss Barrow lying in the bed, asleep, snoring loudly, Margaret Seddon dozing fitfully in the chair by her side, Mr Seddon and Ernie Grant each alone in their respective beds.

As the sky outside began to lighten with the approach of dawn, Frederick Seddon made his way once more up the stairs to visit his wife in her uncomfortable vigil. Soon he was drawing her attention to a marked change in the patient. Her loud snoring and heavy breathing had stopped. Bending over the bed, he lifted her eyelids.

'Good God,' he said, 'she's dead.'

Later that same day, nine-year-old Ernie Grant was sent away to Southend for a holiday. He was told nothing of the death of the woman who had devotedly looked after him ever since he became an orphan five years before and whom he had always called 'Chicky'. Dr Sworn, once more consulted, saw no reason to doubt that the death had been anything but natural. He therefore issued a certificate giving the cause of death as 'epidemic diarrhoea and general exhaustion'.

As will have been gathered from her comfortable financial position, Miss Barrow was by no means a member of the 'lower orders'. There was a family vault in Highgate Cemetery. In it lay both her parents, together with a number of other close relatives, and it was there that she assumed she would, one day, finally be 'laid to rest'. Of this, Seddon was well aware. Papers relating to it were in her possession and she occasionally referred to it. And yet, on the very morning of her death, Frederick Seddon entered the office of William Knowles, an undertaker in Stroud Green Road, and negotiated a cheap funeral for her.

He explained to Mr Knowles that an old lady had died in his house, only £4.10s had been found to belong to her; the doctor's fees had to be paid out of that. Mr Knowles helpfully suggested that he provide a funeral for only £4. Seddon, however, replied that the remaining 10s would be insufficient to pay the doctor's fees. After delicate negotiations it was finally agreed that Miss Barrow be given a funeral costing the princely sum of £3-7s-6d. Seddon would, however, be given a receipt for £4, the difference being his commission.

For this extravagant sum Mr Knowles would supply a coffin, polished and ornamented, complete with handles. There would be a composite carriage, that is, a carriage that conveyed both the coffin and the mourners, the coffin being hidden from view below the carriage floor. There would also be the necessary bearers. Obviously, for such a small sum she could not expect to have a grave of her own. She would be buried in a common grave, together with five or six other unfortunate male and female paupers, in Islington cemetery.

It was further agreed with the sympathetic and understanding Mr Knowles that it would 'look bad' to have a pauper's funeral begin in the highly respectable precincts of Tollington Park. That very morning, the mortal remains of Miss Barrow were discreetly transferred to the premises of Mr Knowles in Stroud Green Road. And it was from there that, only two days after her death, the funeral procession conveying Miss Barrow set out for her far from lonely grave. Not that there was much of a procession, just the one carriage. Seddon had said nothing to Mr Knowles about providing carriages for mourners. But then, there were no mourners, apart that is from Mr and Mrs Seddon.

But what of her relatives? What of her cousins living only a couple of streets away? Why did they not attend the funeral? Because they had not been told that she was ill, they had not been told that she was dead, and now they had not been told of her funeral.

In the days immediately following Miss Barrow's death, Seddon was a very busy man. On the same day as her death he had arranged for her quiet funeral. That same afternoon two of his assistants came to his office in the basement of his Tollington Park home. This was a perfectly routine arrangement, during which the week's takings were added up and the necessary paperwork prepared for submission to their employers.

One of the men, Harry Taylor, spent most of the afternoon there. Seeing that Seddon looked rather tired and being informed that he and his wife had been up half the night attending to a sick woman, Mr Taylor kindly suggested that Seddon should go and lie down for a while. This Seddon did, leaving his assistant to organize the paperwork. After a few hours he returned to his office where Mr Taylor was busy balancing the accounts. As the visitor was working, he heard the clinking of coins. Glancing across to Seddon's desk he was surprised to see his companion with a pile of gold coins. He was counting them up and building them into neat little piles before transfering them to variously coloured paper bags. Mr Taylor, with a professional eye, estimated their value as being well over £200. The total takings for the business that week had amounted to £63-14s-3d, almost entirely in silver.

The next day, 15 September, Seddon paid a visit to Thomas Bright, a jeweller in the nearby Holloway Road. He produced a gentleman's single-stone diamond ring which he said he wanted enlarged. The same day he called at the shop again, this time with a watch. He wished to have a gold dial substituted for the existing enamel one and also asked that the inscription 'E.J. Barrow 1860' be deleted. On this second occasion his wife was with him. Miss Barrow had been dead a little over twenty-four hours.

Also on that same day he paid £30 into the Post Office Savings Bank, an amount equivalent to over ten weeks' salary. He then paid £90 in gold for shares in a building society. The day after he went back to the building society with a further £90 for more shares.

While all this activity was going on around Tollington Park Miss Barrow's relatives, who were now living only four hundred yards away in Corbyn Street, remained in total ignorance of their cousin's demise. But it was not an ignorance that could be expected to last forever. A small son of the Vanderahes' attended the same school as Ernest Grant. He was soon conveying the news to his parents that Ernie was not at school. A school inspector went round to Tollington Park to discover the reason for the boy's absence. 'He is ill,' was the explanation given.

On the 18th Mr Vanderahe, passing along Tollington Park, was amazed to see that all the windows on the top floor of number 63 were wide open. Miss Barrow was, in his experience, always complaining of draughts even when the windows were shut; the possibility of her allowing them to be wide open was very unlikely indeed. Mr and Mrs Vanderahe discussed the matter and decided that they had better find out just what was going on.

Two days later, in search of answers, Frank Vanderahe made his way to 63 Tollington Park, mounted the front steps and rang the bell. The door was opened by the Seddon's servant, Mary Chater, with a child in her arms.

'Can I see Miss Barrow?' he asked.

The girl's reaction was not at all what he had expected. She was clearly taken aback, for a moment speechless, then said:

'Don't you know that she is dead and buried?'

He, of course, did not know. When he had recovered from his own surprise, he pressed the girl for more information. She told him that Miss Barrow had been buried the previous Saturday. She said that if he wished to know more it would be best for him to call back in about an hour, when the master would have returned. He did call back in an hour, but did not see Frederick Seddon. Indeed it was only when he returned for the third time that that gentleman condescended to put in an appearance.

The meeting, when at last it did take place, was not a success. Seddon claimed that he had written to them, telling them of the woman's death and notifying them of the funeral arrangements. When challenged as to why she was buried at Islington and not in the family vault at Highgate, Seddon said that he thought that the vault was full up. He did not disclose that she was in a pauper's grave.

The next morning Mrs Julia Vanderahe, together with her sister-in-law, Mrs Amelia Vanderahe, went to Tollington Park determined to learn more. The door was opened by young Maggie Seddon. She showed them into the sitting-room where they found themselves facing Mrs Seddon as well as her husband. Mr Seddon spoke of the night when Miss Barrow died and said that his wife had been worn out by it. He produced a copy of a letter which he claimed to have posted to them:

I sincerely regret to have to inform you of the death of your cousin Miss Eliza Mary Barrow at 6 a.m. this morning, from epidemic diarrhoea. The funeral will take place on Saturday next at about 1 or 2p.m. Please inform Albert, Edward and Emma Vanderahe of her decease and let me know if you wish to attend the funeral. I must also inform you that she made a will on the 11th instant leaving what she died possessed of to Hilda and Ernest Grant and appointed myself as sole Executor under the will.

Asked about the funeral, Mrs Seddon assured them that it had been 'a nice one'. The two women were then shown the will. They were not impressed. It was written in pencil. When pressed, Seddon said that it was, of course, only a copy. Julia declared her intention of going to Somerset House and inspecting the original. Seddon replied that it would be a waste of time, it would not be there. He had spoken to the officials and they had told him that it would not be necessary to prove the will.

The two Vanderahe women were not, however, fools. The more they heard, the less they liked what they heard. They asked that Seddon tell them at what time the next day it would be convenient for him to see their husbands. Seddon replied that he and his family were about to go on holiday and could not spare the time. The following morning they did indeed go away to the coast for a fortnight's holiday.

But if Seddon believed that he could shake off the Vanderahe family as easily as that, he was deluding himself. Shortly after his return on 9 October, he was visited by Frank Vanderahe, together with a friend performing the function of a witness. In no uncertain manner they demanded admittance.

'What do you want?' asked a less than friendly Seddon.

'I have called to see the will of my cousin and also the policy,' he was told.

Seddon reluctantly allowed them into the house.

'I do not know why I should give you information,' he said. 'You are not the eldest of the family. You have another brother of the name of Percy.'

'Yes, but he might be dead for all I know.'

'I do not know that I should show you. Everything is perfectly legal, Miss Barrow did everything herself.'

'Who is the owner of the Bucks Head now?'

'I am, likewise the barber's shop next door. I am always open to buy property. This house I live in, fourteen rooms, is my own and I have seventeen properties. I am always open to buy property at a price.'

'Who bought the India stock?'

'You had better ask the Bank of England.'

By now the Vanderahe family was smelling a very large rat. Upon returning from their meeting with Seddon they all discussed the whole affair and then wrote to the Department of Public Prosecutions. The authorities, with their customary caution, made enquiries of their own. They, too, became increasingly suspicious and curious about the sudden death, the precipitous and strangely secret funeral and the convenient will. An application was made and granted for an exhumation order. On 15 November, two months after her burial, the body of Miss Barrow was lifted from the ground and taken away for an overdue post-mortem.

Dr Wilcox, who conducted the examination, was immediately struck by the amazing condition of the body. After two months' interment it was in a quite remarkable state of preservation. Almost no decay at all. The reason soon became evident, the whole body was absolutely saturated with arsenic. Not only did they discover arsenic in her stomach, clearly indicating the cause of death, but it was present in every part of her body, even in the extremities of her fingernails. This could only mean that the unfortunate woman had been ingesting the poison over a long period. The final dose, judging by the amount still remaining in her stomach, must have been a massive one.

On 23 November a formal inquest was opened at Friern Barnet, into the death of Eliza Mary Barrow, before the Coroner for Central Middlesex, Dr George Cohen. The packed court was told of the peculiar circumstances surrounding the woman's death and of the curious manner in which her funeral was conducted. They heard from the Vanderahe family of their fruitless attempts to discover the facts behind the disposal of their cousin's possessions and of their growing suspicions. Finally they were told by Dr Wilcox of the exhumation of the body, of its remarkable state of preservation and of the discovery in it of a substantial quantity of arsenic. The inquest was then adjourned for three weeks to enable further investigations to be made.

But much was to happen before that event took place. Amongst the crowd of people packed into the coroner's court, listening intently to every word, was Detective Chief-Inspector Wood. At seven o'clock on the evening of Monday, 4 December, Frederick Seddon left his house and began to walk along Tollington Park. Whatever his intentions had been, he was not to walk very far. Only a short distance from his home his further progress was stopped by Chief-Inspector Wood:

'I am a police officer,' he told Seddon, 'and shall arrest you for the wilful murder of Eliza Mary Barrow by means of poison, arsenic.'

Seddon was highly indignant to be stopped and arrested, here in the street in front of the neighbours. It was absolutely scandalous.

'Absurd. What a terrible charge, wilful murder. It is the first of our family that has ever been accused of such a crime. Are you going to arrest my wife as well? If not, I would like you to give her a message from me. Have they found arsenic in her body?'

'She did not do this herself.'

'It was not carbolic acid was it, as there was some of it in her room? Sanitas is not a poison, is it?'

When the inquest resumed on 14 December the court was able to hear evidence given by that most famous of Home Office pathologists, Dr Bernard Spilsbury.

> I think that the extremely marked preservation of the body, taking into consideration the time of the year at which death occurred and the period which had elapsed between death and my examination, renders it improbable that death was due to natural gastro-enteritis or summer diarrhoea and that death was due rather to the action of some poison which had a preservative effect.

> If you had been told that a body with all the appearances of this body had been found and that there was arsenic in the body, what would you say death was due to?

> Arsenical poisoning.

Arsenic was found in all the organs and tissues of the body. The largest amount was in the intestines, stomach, liver and muscles. There was also arsenic in the skin, hair and nails. Spilsbury estimated that he had traced 2.01 grains which suggested that she must have taken about five grains. Two grains would have been sufficient to have caused death. Asked by the coroner whether, during his examination of the body, he had found any disease which could account for the woman's death, he replied:

> I found no evidence of disease except for slight reddening of the surface of the intestines and stomach which would be consistent with epidemical diarrhoea.

Mr and Mrs Seddon were both closely questioned about the arrangements for preparing Miss Barrow's meals and medicines. Mrs Seddon said that she had nursed Miss Barrow throughout her last illness, that she had prepared the woman's food and medicine and that her husband had on only two occasions been in the sick woman's

159

room and then not alone. After the customary deliberation, the coroner's jury declared their considered verdict:

> We unanimously find that the deceased died on the 14th September 1911, from arsenical poisoning, feloniously adminis-tered, but sufficient evidence is not before us to enable us to decide by whom it was administered.

One month later, on 15 January 1912, Mrs Margaret Seddon was also arrested and charged with wilful murder.

The Old Bailey trial, held before Mr Justice Bucknill, began on 4 March and lasted all of ten days. The prosecution was conducted by the Attorney-General, Sir Rufus Isaacs, the defence by Marshall Hall. Formidable advocates in both meanings of the term.

The evidence against the Seddons was entirely circumstantial, but that is hardly surprising; no one in his right mind administers poison in front of witnesses. If you have a woman living in your house, however, who, over a period of more than a week does not leave her room, is entirely dependent upon you for her food and medicine and who then dies from a massive dose of arsenic, it is rather difficult to argue that it has nothing to do with you.

Throughout the length of the trial Frederick and Margaret Seddon sat in the dock together. From time to time Frederick whispered a comment to his wife and received in return a nod or quiet comment. But to the occupants of the public gallery, to the press and to the jury, the two prisoners made totally different impressions.

From her very first appearance in court, the newspapers were writing of Margaret Seddon as having a graceful dignity, of being refined and cultured, of having an attractive face and figure. Her husband, on the other hand, made a completely different impression. He came over as cold and calculating, wholly aloof, totally unmoved by anything that he heard, apparently devoid of human feeling.

His appearance and manner of replying to questions helped to give this impression:

'What security had Miss Barrow that you would continue to pay this annuity?' he was asked.

'My personal obligation to pay. I was getting financially stronger every day. Isn't any financial strength security? Isn't a legal document security?'

Questioned about having been seen counting a large number of sovereigns on the same day as Miss Barrow's death, he replied:

'I am not a degenerate. That would make out that I am a greedy inhuman monster. The suggestion is scandalous. I would have had all day to count the money.'

The major questions that had to be answered were those of the provenance of the arsenic and how it got into Miss Barrow's body.

The prosecution alleged that the arsenic had been obtained from flypapers. They had tests carried out which proved that boiling or even just soaking flypapers in water was quite sufficient to remove the arsenic and produce a potentially lethal dose. Each flypaper contained more than enough arsenic to kill an adult and the Seddons had purchased a packet of six. Arsenic is tasteless and colourless. Obtained from the flypapers, it would colour the water in which it was dissolved but this problem could easily be solved by mixing it with the meat extract that Miss Barrow was known to have been given. It could equally well be used to make tea.

Frederick Seddon naturally denied ever having obtained arsenic in such a way:

'I have never known anybody to do it until I heard in this court that it had been done by experiment.'

The defence tried to argue that, since the normal method of using flypapers to kill flies involved placing a paper in a saucer of water, Miss Barrow, feeling suddenly thirsty, might have removed the flypaper and drunk the water. The jury, however, is likely to have thought that, while Miss Barrow may well have been eccentric, she was unlikely to have been that eccentric.

There was also a rare moment of humour. Defence counsel, hearing that Miss Barrow had been given bismuth as part of her medicine and that bismuth contained arsenic, suggested that that might have led to her death. Dr Spilsbury was asked how much bismuth it would require to obtain the fatal dose of two grains of arsenic:

'About two hundredweight,' he replied.

When, at the end of the ten days, the jury was asked to give its verdict, they produced a very popular but decidedly strange one. They declared Frederick Seddon 'Guilty' but Margaret Seddon 'Not Guilty'.

These verdicts were decidedly peculiar because there was much more evidence against Margaret Seddon than there was against her husband. Who was it, after all, who nursed Miss Barrow? Who was it who prepared her food? Who was it who gave her her medicine? Who was it who would not allow Mary Chater to do anything on the top floor of the house? In every case the answer is Margaret Seddon.

And yet, not only was she allowed to go free but was viewed by almost everyone with sympathy as an innocent wife suffering because of the wickedness of her husband.

The discrepancy between the two verdicts was, no doubt, given partly because of the very different impressions made by the two defendants in the dock. But, it was also the case that, in 1911, women were still viewed as creatures that were simple-minded but inherently good. Add to that the normal class bias of the time and you produce a situation in which it was taken to be a self-evident fact that a charming cultivated woman could not possibly commit cold-blooded murder.

Before we take our final leave of the Seddon case, there is one very interesting piece of evidence which was completely overlooked at their trial and which throws new light upon their guilt. It comes from Frederick's reply to the allegation of obtaining arsenic from flypapers:

'I have never known anybody to do it until I heard in this court that it had been done by experiment.'

Now, that really is rather curious because the technique was by no means new. Twenty-two years earlier, in 1889, Mrs Maybrick, the wife of a Liverpool cotton-merchant, used precisely that method to obtain the arsenic which she then fatally administered to her husband. Of that there was no doubt, a servant saw her doing it.

But what reason is there for supposing that either of the Seddons of Tollington Park, north London, knew anything about a crime committed twenty-two years earlier in Liverpool?

The clue comes from a newspaper report of the trial which described Mrs Seddon as having 'a slight Lancashire accent'. So, where exactly in Lancashire did Margaret Seddon come from? The answer is in their marriage certificate. It records the marriage between Frederick Henry Seddon and Margaret Ann Jones on 31 December 1893 at St George's Church, Everton. They both lived in the same road, Priory Street. They were both Liverpudlians.

The Maybrick case was the most sensational murder ever committed on Merseyside. It filled the Liverpool papers for months, it dominated conversation in the city. It is quite inconceivable that anyone living in Liverpool and over the age of ten could not know of Mrs Maybrick and the way by which she murdered her husband. At the time, Frederick Seddon was seventeen and Margaret Jones fourteen.

There can be no real doubt that the Seddons remembered the

story of Mrs Maybrick and used her technique to kill Miss Barrow. There can be no real doubt that Frederick Seddon was rightfully convicted and hanged for wilful murder. There can equally be no real doubt that Margaret Seddon, quite literally, got away with murder.

THE MUSIC
TEACHER

THE MUSIC
TEACHER

High up on a ridge of chalk cliffs, overlooking the Thames estuary, stands the Kent village of Northfleet. During the last years of Victoria's reign it provided a grandstand view of the world's shipping. Steamships of all shapes and sizes, from small coasters to ocean liners, men of war and the last great generation of sailing-ships: barques, brigantines, schooners and Thames sailing barges in their hundreds, looking with their great red sails like clouds of enormous butterflies upon the water. A panoramic view of the hub of a great empire.

It was here, with such a sight close to her doorstep, that Mary Jane Clarke grew up, the daughter of a butcher. She was born on 28 September 1877 and was her parents' pride and joy.

Clearly taking their duties seriously they gave her a good education and, thanks to financial assistance from her grandparents, special attention was given to her music, a subject in which she was clearly talented. While still a young girl she performed on local concert platforms and, by the time she was in her teens, appeared occasionally at a Gravesend theatre.

At the age of seventeen, encouraged to make use of her talents, she placed advertisements in a local newspaper, offering music lessons for both piano and violin. Amongst her new pupils was Herbert John Bennett who enrolled to study the violin. Two years her junior, he was later to be described as 'having a good forehead, wavy dark-brown hair, a long nose which is straight except for a slight tilt just at the end; brown eyes, rather too close together, large unshapely ears, slightly receding chin and a small moustache, twisted upwards'. He also seems to have developed, at an unusually early age, a great deal of charm and the knowledge of how to use it. This last quality, coupled with the ability to talk convincingly, was, in the end, to lead to his downfall.

For her part, Mary Clarke does not seem to have been a particularly attractive girl, being 5' 2" tall, with bronze-coloured shoulder-length hair; she normally wore glasses and, rather curiously for a music teacher, was somewhat deaf.

Place a young inexperienced girl in close proximity to an attractive young man and the result is not entirely unpredictable. She fell in love with him. When, before very long, they approached her parents with talk of marriage the response was equally predictable. The whole idea of her marrying a Co-op shop assistant earning 15s a week was quite clearly ridiculous and, in any case, they were both far too young.

It was not long before her parents had to reconsider their position, however, as the affair continued to follow its course. Mary Clarke became pregnant. The position of an unmarried mother is never easy; in the 1890s, especially for respectable people like the Clarkes, it was unthinkable. In spite of continued opposition from Herbert's parents, on the grounds that he was still only seventeen, the marriage did indeed take place. But it was not at all the kind of marriage that Mr and Mrs Clarke had planned for their daughter: the bride looking radiant in front of admiring neighbours, followed by a 'good spread' and jollifications. The ceremony did not even take place at Northfleet but at a registry office at West Ham, near her grandparents' home, on 22 July 1897.

The young couple lived for a while with her parents, a clearly uncomfortable situation, especially as, soon after the marriage, Herbert lost his job with Northfleet Co-operative Stores and, at least in the eyes of his father-in-law, did not seem very interested in finding another. He appeared to be content simply to wander about the marshes with a shotgun.

Their first child died soon after birth, a common enough occurrence in those days. After a while, to relieve the obvious tension between Herbert and his father-in-law, the young couple moved to West Ham and lived with Mary's grandmother. When she died, in April 1898, the old lady left her grand-daughter the gold necklace which she had long admired. This, together with the silver watch given to her by her father on her twelfth birthday, she was to wear for the rest of her short life.

The death of her grandmother also resulted in a violent quarrel between her husband and her father over ownership of the old lady's furniture. During the course of this, Bennett threatened his father-in-law with a gun. After that incident all contact between the Bennetts and the Clarkes seems to have ended. There also seems to have been very little communication between Bennett and his own father.

Over the next few years, Mr and Mrs Bennett lived by running a series of 'businesses'. This usually involved buying goods on credit, selling them for cash and then not paying their suppliers. Naturally, this meant that they had to move rather frequently and change their names fairly often. Having, by this effective if dubious means, acquired some capital, they were soon running a small greengrocery and coal business in the south London district of Battersea. But even this did not operate like a normal business. The local people were greatly puzzled by it. The shop seemed to be hardly ever open although the owners could frequently be seen proceeding together through the streets of Battersea, in regal style, with a horse and cart.

The explanation for this strange behaviour is that Herbert Bennett was, as he described it, 'trading in violins'. This method of business was simple and highly profitable, if considerably less than honest. It meant purchasing cheap, through *Exchange & Mart*, a job lot of second-hand violins of dubious quality. Mary Bennett then sold them. She did this by posing as the poverty-stricken widow of a professional musician who had been struck down in the prime of life. Being left, broken-hearted and destitute with small children to fend for, she was forced to sell the only thing she had of any value, her dead husband's beloved violin. Generous, soft-hearted housewives, faced by this pale and tearful young woman, standing rain-soaked on their doorsteps with a child in her arms, paid for the violins far more than they were worth.

By this means the Bennetts became quite prosperous, though what Mary's parents would have thought of their daughter's behaviour can easily be imagined. Throughout their period of living in Battersea their neighbours never once heard Mary play either the piano or violin, although they frequently heard Herbert 'try to play the violin', as they put it; this sounds rather painful. It was while they were resident in Battersea that their daughter Ruby was born in October 1898.

This newly acquired wealth, coupled with the urgent need to once more move to pastures new, resulted in the Bennetts becoming ambitious and purchasing a grocer's shop at Westgate-on-Sea. The asking price for the business was £450, of which Bennett paid £375 in cash and the balance in bills. Whether Bennett ever had any real intention of becoming a normal shop-keeper is by no means clear although, given his character, it does seem rather unlikely. In any event, only two months after its purchase, the shop suffered a mysterious fire and was completely destroyed. The Kent Insurance Company initially refused to pay for the fire damage but eventually compromised with a payment of £285.

Early in March 1900 Bennett, together with his wife, paid a rare visit to his grandparents in Gravesend and asked them to look after the baby as they were going to North America. This they agreed to do and, on 7 March, he purchased steamer tickets. They were not, however, for North America but for Cape Town. He booked a two-berth cabin on the SS *Gaika* in the names of Mr and Mrs Hood, paying £45 in notes. Before sailing he visited a London theatre-costumery where he bought a wig and a false moustache for himself and a blond wig for his wife. Their period in Cape Town was remarkably short, only four days, and by 9 May they were back in England. The purpose of this curious escapade is unknown but it should be born in mind that the Boer War was taking place at the time and the suggestion has been made that he was hoping to spy for the Boers. It can safely be assumed that, whatever the motive for the trip, it is unlikely to have been honest.

On 9 May they took rooms at the home of Mrs Emma Elliston, the wife of a police constable, at 64 Wickham Lane, Plumstead, a large semi-detached house overlooking open fields. Here we find their marriage under stress. As Mrs Elliston was later to testify, while Mary Bennett was always loving and affectionate towards her husband, constantly calling him 'dear' and 'dearest', he was frequently violent and foul-mouthed to her. On one occasion, during a quarrel, Mary was heard to say to her husband, 'Herbert, I shall always follow you for the sake of the child and if you are not careful I will get you fifteen years.' Herbert replied to this curious mixture of threat and promise by declaring that he wished she were dead and, if she wasn't careful, she soon would be. Whether either of them really believed what they were saying, or were just having a fairly normal matrimonial quarrel, we shall never know, but what we do know is that, almost immediately, Herbert Bennett began to lead a double-life.

Mary Bennett took rooms at 10 Woolwich Road while her husband, from 12 June, lived at 41 Union Street, Woolwich, where he posed as a single man. But, for Mary at least, this was only a temporary arrangement for quite soon she was renting a small house, 1 Glencoe Villa, Izane Road, Bexley Heath. To obtain this recently built, semi-detached house it was necessary for her to provide a suitable reference. She was able to meet this requirement with very little difficulty:

> 61 High Street,
> Putney.

At Mrs Bennett's request, as she tells me it is your wish that I should, I give her this reference to give you personally.

She has been my tenant for a period of five years at £36 per year, and I have found her to be a respectable and careful tenant, and I can thoroughly recommend her as a suitable & respectable tenant to you at the rate she mentioned to me of 8/- per week.
> Yours faithfully,
> W.A. Phillips

It was only learned a great deal later that this certificate of respectability was written by her husband.

While living at Glencoe Villa Mary was visited infrequently by her husband. During one of these rare appearances he was overheard to complain, 'You are always dragging money out of me, you know the fix I'm in now.' He was at this time employed with the Woolwich Co-operative Stores but left them on 29 June and was unemployed until 16 July when he started work as a general labourer in Woolwich Arsenal at 30s a week. He was living under the name of W.H. Bennett.

In August Mary was taken ill and sent a telegram to her husband which he explained to his landlady, Mrs Parkhurst, as having come from his cousin Fred's family at Bexley. He was to become very fond of his 'cousin Fred' over the next few months.

At Mrs Parkhurst's Bennett shared a room with another lodger, a man called Stevens. Early in July Stevens, believing Bennett to be a single man, introduced him to a young parlour-maid, Alice Meadows, who was employed by a family near Hyde Park. They quickly became very friendly, frequently 'walking out' together and exchanging letters. Although he described himself to her as being an unemployed shop-assistant he always seemed to have plenty of money and they were soon discussing the possibilities of holidaying in Ireland together.

Alice, being a sensible girl, was somewhat cautious about offers of holidays from men that she did not know very well. Bennett suggested that, before venturing to Ireland, they should have a weekend in Yarmouth. One of Alice's fellow employees knew of some suitable addresses in Yarmouth and Bennett was soon writing to a Mrs Rudrum of 3 Row 104 at that resort. Mrs Rudrum, however, quickly replied that, as it was a bank-holiday weekend, she had no accommodation free.

In spite of that, Herbert Bennett and Alice Meadows travelled first-class to Yarmouth on 4 August where they stayed at the Crown & Anchor Hotel, having separate rooms.

During their holiday they walked through 'the Rows'. When, thanks to its fishing industry, the town first began to grow in economic strength it faced a problem of space. The site of the town having originated as little more than a sand-bank, there was a severe shortage of land upon which to build a town. The Rows were the result. They were a unique network of narrow lanes, 129 of them, some so narrow that it was possible to stand in the centre of the road and touch both sides. In their explorations of this fascinating area they saw the Rudrum's home and Bennett commented how horrible it would have been to have stayed there rather than at their pleasant hotel.

The weekend proved successful, they had a nice holiday and Alice's doubts were dispelled. At the end of August they travelled together to Ireland and spent a fortnight in the romantic atmosphere of Killarney. Money appeared to be no problem, they stayed in hotels, travelled first-class, Bennett was always the perfect gentleman and, by the time that they returned to England on 11 September, Alice was the proud possessor of a diamond-and-ruby ring.

It was agreed that the marriage should take place the following June. A few days later, on 14 September, Bennett paid one of his rare visits to his wife at Bexley Heath. Not long after his departure, Mary went out shopping with a neighbour, Lilian Langman. Although Mary said nothing, Mrs Langman gained the impression that she was going away. She purchased a number of items of clothing, including a blouse and a veil.

That same Friday, the 14th, Bennett told Alice Meadows that he would not be able to see her the following day because he had to visit his grandfather who had been taken ill at his home in Gravesend.

On the morning of Saturday, 15 September, after having arranged to have the day off work because of illness, Bennett once more visited his wife and child. Upon his leaving, Mary immediately packed a suitcase and, after telling Mrs Langman that she was going to Leeds, asked her to look after her dog. She then locked up the house and, taking little Ruby with her, left for Yarmouth, never to return.

At nine o'clock that evening a Mrs Hood, together with a two-year-old girl with blue eyes and long blond hair, arrived at Mrs Rudrum's house in Yarmouth. Although she arrived alone Mr Rudrum, a shoemaker, thought that he saw her at the end of the alley with a man. Given the notorious difficulties strangers had in finding their way through the maze of alleyways that constituted the Rows, especially after dark, it was certain that she must have had clear directions to the house from someone.

Remaining there only long enough to leave her luggage and put the child to bed, Mrs Hood immediately went out again, not returning until nearly midnight. When she once more entered the house she had quite obviously been drinking and explained that she had been with her brother-in-law.

During her stay in Yarmouth she developed the habit of going out every evening, after having put the child to bed, but was always back by nine o'clock. She told Mrs Rudrum that she was twenty-seven and that her husband had died just before the child was born. She also confided to the sympathetic Mrs Rudrum that her brother-in-law was in love with her and was very jealous.

The same night that the widowed Mrs Hood arrived in Yarmouth, Herbert Bennett booked in at the Crown & Anchor and left early the next morning, catching the 7.30 a.m. train. It arrived in London at 11.30 and, by midday, he had turned up unexpectedly at 22 York Road, Stepney, the home of Alice Meadows's mother.

On Wednesday, the 19th, Bennett called at Glencoe Villa, did not enter but asked if anyone had been there. The next day he told Alice that he would, once more, be unable to meet her on Sunday as he would again be visiting his sick grandfather at Gravesend. During the afternoon of Saturday, 22 September, his landlady, Mrs Parkhurst, met him in Union Street not far from her home. She noticed that he was carrying a railway timetable.

On the evening of Friday, the 21st, Mrs Hood received a letter, postmarked Woolwich, saying 'Meet me under the big clock and put your baby to bed.' It was signed 'Hood'. This was explained to Mrs Rudrum and her daughter as emanating from her brother-in-law who was trying to find a house for her in London.

The following evening, Saturday the 22nd, Mrs Hood left the house much as usual, wearing her gold necklace and silver watch. Between 8.30 and 9 p.m. she was seen standing outside the Town Hall, apparently waiting for someone. At about ten o'clock she entered the bar of the South Quay Distillery with a man. As the bar was normally used only by the local fishermen and their wives, the two well-dressed strangers were somewhat conspicuous. The man drank whiskies, the woman gin and the landlord, Mr Barking, could not help noticing that the man, who sported a surprisingly large moustache, kept touching it in a very odd manner. As the woman sat, sipping her drink, the man consulted a railway timetable. After some time, they left together.

Late that evening a Yarmouth moulder, Alfred Marks, lay on the beach with his young lady, Blanche Smith, enjoying those pleasures usually indulged in by young couples on dark beaches. It was a dark, moonless night, but dry and quite warm. Suddenly, from somewhere not far away, there came a scuffling in the sand. A single cry of 'Mercy' from a woman and then silence. The two young people sat there, listening intently, hearing nothing, until, with the characteristic discretion of the English, they decided not to make fools of themselves by intervening and returned to their pleasures. Not long afterwards they walked hand-in-hand along that part of the beach. They saw and heard nothing apart from the gentle murmur of the sea.

Shortly before midnight a man arrived at the Crown & Anchor Hotel. He was out of breath and rather dishevelled which he explained as being caused by his just missing the last tram from Gorleston. He did not give a name but the waiter, named Read, recognized him as being the Mr Bennett who had stayed there with the young woman in August. The man explained that he had to make occasional business trips to Yarmouth. He said that he was particularly anxious to catch the first London train in the morning and asked for an early call. He was accordingly woken early and left for the station in time to catch the 7.20 a.m. train.

A local newsagent, Mr Headley, saw him shortly before the train left. He was standing at the open door of a third-class compartment in what appeared to Mr Headley to be 'a nervous and agitated condition'. He was dressed 'in a light grey suit and one of those soft trilby hats'.

Soon after 6.30 a.m. on the morning of Sunday, 23 September, fourteen-year-old John Lawton left his home at 36 Boreham Road and turned down Barrack Road towards the sea. It was one of those days, all too common on the east coast of England, when a grey sky meets a grey sea with scarcely a line to show their meeting. So early on a Sunday morning most of Yarmouth was still asleep. Even the sea seemed hardly awake, small waves half-heartedly tickling the shore, with scarcely a murmur. Reaching the area by the sea known as South Denes he set off at an angle across the beach towards the group of bathing-huts that was his destination, his shoes sinking deep into the fine, dry sand. As he did so, he noticed a woman apparently asleep on the beach.

When he reached the bathing-huts he met Mr Briers who maintained them. Having said 'Good morning' and exchanged comments about the weather in the approved English way, he mentioned the sleeping woman. People sleeping on the beach were by no means unusual at Yarmouth, although it was greatly frowned upon by the local council. Mr Briers suggested to him that 'he better go and wake her up'.

The young lad retraced his steps across the sands to where the woman still lay motionless. He spoke to her but received no response. He then knelt down and gently shook her by the shoulder but quickly discovered that she was dead. He was soon on his feet, running for help. Heading for town, he came across P.C. Manship, just coming on duty and, between gasps for breath, explained his discovery. Showing the professional caution of not believing anything until he had seen it for himself, the constable walked back with him to the beach. He had a quick look to establish that the woman really was dead, saw that the cause of her death made it a case of murder and immediately set the official wheels turning.

The woman was lying on her back with her hands by her sides, her fingers clenched, her skirt and petticoat above her knees. There were scratches on her face and a mohair bootlace round her neck, so tight that the flesh overlapped it, making it difficult even to cut. Closer examination of the body revealed traces of sand on the tip of her tongue, probably caused by her assailant's hand being held over her mouth to enforce silence.

She was wearing a dove-coloured skirt and a jacket trimmed with white braid, also a white blouse with a green tie. Lying by her side was a white sailor hat which had a black band and a black veil with white spots. In her pocket was a pair of kid gloves. Her hair, which hung loose upon her shoulders, was bronze at the roots but had been dyed a golden colour. On the third finger of her left hand she wore three rings, with two more on the third finger of her right hand. She had neither bracelet nor watch.

Mrs Rudrum had already reported the disappearance of one of her guests. The police soon put the two cases together and searched the room and luggage of the mysterious Mrs Hood. For mysterious, Mrs Hood proved to be. Apart from a return railway-ticket from Liverpool Street and the laundry mark 599 on some of the baby's linen, they could find nothing to indicate where she came from. The letter from Woolwich was missing, as was her watch and bracelet. The police did find in her room, however, a picture of her and her child taken a few days earlier by one of the local beach photographers. They began to distribute copies of this over a wide area in the hope that someone would recognize her and come forward.

At the end of October the police had made no further progress on the case and the coroner's jury passed a verdict of 'wilful murder by person or persons unknown'. After a funeral service, which the police deliberately kept secret to keep away sightseers, but whose small congregation included Mrs Rudrum and her daughter Alice, Mrs Hood was buried in the churchyard of St Nicholas watched by a large crowd.

Meanwhile, back in Woolwich, Herbert Bennett was very busy. On Wednesday, 26 September, he visited Glencoe Villa and afterwards went to the house agents intending to terminate the lease on the house. He was told that he must write and give notice in the proper manner. That same day he met Alice Meadows, telling her that his grandfather had died and that his cousin Fred was taking his family to South Africa. He said that he had arranged to buy their furniture and that he wished to marry her by Christmas. He wanted to get settled down as soon as possible. He gave her some of his wife's clothing, saying that it belonged to his cousin's wife who would not want heavy clothing in South Africa. He also gave her a brooch, shaped in the form of a pick and shovel, which belonged to his wife.

He wrote to the house agents confirming his wish to end the tenancy on Glencoe Villa and giving the necessary three months' notice. He explained to them that Mrs Bennett had gone away for health reasons. The lease was eventually ended early, upon payment of £4-10s.

At about this time he accidentally met in the street a Mr Parritt who knew him to be a married man. In response to the normal questions about the health of his family, he replied that his wife and child had both died in South Africa and that it upset him to talk about it.

On 6 October he went once more to Bexley Heath where he collected his wife's dog from Mrs Langman, telling her that he was taking it to his wife who was ill in Leeds.

For six weeks the police had worked at identifying the woman found murdered on Yarmouth beach. Her photograph had been widely distributed, from time to time someone had come forward believing that they might know her identity, but always there was disappointment. Policemen had spent many hours visiting countless laundries in fruitless attempts to find number 599. But, for all their efforts, they had achieved nothing.

Then, early in November, their dogged persistence finally paid off. They traced the laundry mark. It was identified as relating to linen emanating from 1 Glencoe Villa, Bexley Heath. Enquiries amongst the neighbours revealed that a Mrs Bennett had been living there with a small child, but that she had not been seen for some time. The beach photograph was shown and quickly identified. Mrs Hood and Mrs Bennett were, indeed, the same woman. A few more days of asking questions and then a man named Allen told them where they could find Mr Bennett.

On 8 November Chief-Inspector Leach went to Woolwich and saw Herbert Bennett. He showed Bennett the beach photograph. Bennett studied the picture with evident care and said that he was sorry he could not help, but he did not know the woman. When formally arrested he said, 'I don't understand what you mean. I have never been to Yarmouth. I have not lived with my wife since January as I found a lot of letters from another man.'

Searching Bennett's room in his new lodgings at 18 William Street, Woolwich, the police found a portmanteau. It contained, amongst other items, a receipt from the Crown & Anchor Hotel, Yarmouth, dated 6 August, a revolver, a false moustache, a man's wig, a woman's wig and, most damning of all, a long gold necklace and a silver watch.

On 17 November Bennett was brought before Yarmouth magistrates charged with the wilful murder of his wife, Mary. He pleaded 'Not Guilty'. Throughout the four-day hearing he appeared completely relaxed, during the journeys to and from the court frequently smiling for the benefit of the press cameras. Only when the magistrates formally committed him for trial did he show, for a few moments, signs of concern.

It was originally intended to hold the trial as part of the Norfolk County Assizes at Norwich, but his Tunbridge Wells solicitor, E. Elvy Robb, was soon protesting about an East Anglian trial, claiming that his client could not expect a fair trial before a Norfolk jury. He stated that a strong feeling of hostility prevailed against the defendant in Norwich and Great Yarmouth, which was largely attributable to articles in the local press and to a pamphlet which had been extensively circulated in the county; that the defendant as he passed through the streets from the Town Hall to the gaol, had been the subject of bitter and hostile demonstrations.

This led to a long legal discussion during the course of which the Crown Solicitor commented that, while the crime had been committed in Norfolk, it could be argued that it was really a London case; both the victim and defendant came from London, as indeed would most of the witnesses. It was thereupon agreed that the trial be transfered to the Old Bailey.

Accordingly, on 26 February 1901, Herbert John Bennett made his first appearance at the Central Criminal Court before the Lord Chief Justice of England and pleaded, 'Not Guilty'.

Bennett was defended by the great advocate, Marshall Hall, but even he found it difficult to make any headway against the long procession of prosecution witnesses.

There appeared Alice Meadows, 'a slight pale creature, becomingly dressed in black, with a toque of purple velvet trimmed with an ostrich feather', giving evidence against her fiancé on the very day that the banns for her marriage were to have been called.

There appeared William Simmons, Bennett's grandfather, called to deny that he was dead and to answer 'No,' in a clear voice to the question 'and it is not true that you were to be buried on September 24th?'. The *Daily Mail* described him as being 'a grey-haired, feeble old man', the *Evening Standard* as 'hale and hearty'.

Mrs Rudrum appeared to give evidence, including testimony concerning the 'letter from Woolwich'. Marshall Hall questioned her at length as to the colour of the envelope. She had originally called it 'blue' but now said it had been 'blue-grey'. He endeavoured to show that this discrepancy was of vital significance but, in reality, he was just grasping at straws.

According to Bennett, on the night of his wife's murder he was in Woolwich drinking with two young assistants from the Woolwich Co-op, Parrott and Cameron, at Rose's Distillery. The two young men denied this. They confirmed that they frequently did see him there on Saturday nights but, on the evening in question, he was conspicuously absent.

His landlady, Mrs Parkhurst, testified that early the following morning she had gone to his room with a cup of tea, he was not there and his bed had not been slept in.

Then Mr Read, waiter from the Crown & Anchor; the 'boots' from the same hotel; Mr Headley, the newsagent; William Bocking from the South Quay Distillery, together with one of his customers, all swore that they saw Bennett in Yarmouth on the night of the crime or the following morning.

When the time came for Marshall Hall to put the case for the defence, despite all his efforts to portray it as overwhelming it was, in truth, very meagre. He claimed, bitterly and with justification, of 'the venom of the gutter-press'. Before the trial key witnesses had been approached by reporters, masquerading as police officers and demanding statements. Newspapers had published photographs of Bennett with large moustaches superimposed, to prove that he was the man seen in the South Quay Distillery. Large sums of money were offered to witnesses for their stories. But, lamentable though all this was, it did not really alter the clear facts of the case.

Marshall Hall argued that there had been two gold necklaces and that the silver watch found in Bennett's portmanteau was not the silver watch missing from his wife's body. It is unlikely that anyone believed him or, indeed, that he really believed it himself.

A witness was produced to testify that Mary Bennett was not the perfect wife pictured by the prosecution and by the newspapers; that she was often irritating and difficult; that she was greedy and sometimes made nasty remarks to her husband. This was all very well but, even if it were all true, proving that Mary Bennett was no different from anybody else, this would hardly be justification for murdering her.

There remained the very curious evidence given by Mr Sholto Douglas, described as being a gentleman engaged in the fancy-goods trade. Mr Douglas told the court how, on the afternoon of 22 September, he had gone for a long country walk. He was accosted by a man asking for a light; a man who proved extremely difficult to get rid of. A man who claimed that he had recently been to Ireland and was employed at the Woolwich Arsenal.

At Lee Green, where they had a drink together, the mysterious stranger said that there was a namesake of his who kept a nearby barber's shop. He pointed to it. The name above the shop was F.K. Bennett. Mr Douglas said that, while this conversation was taking place, he saw the seven o'clock omnibus leave. The last train for Yarmouth that evening had left Liverpool Street Station at five o'clock. If the story were true, Bennett had an alibi.

But, if it was true, if Herbert Bennett really was the man at Lee Green (and the man in the story did seem to go to a great deal of trouble to create an alibi for himself with his hints as to his identity), why did he not use it? Why did he never mention Mr Sholto Douglas? Why had he not mentioned Lee Green? Even now, in court, he seemed to have been as amazed and baffled by the story as everybody else.

A Yarmouth shopkeeper told a curious story of a shabbily dressed stranger, with a large moustache and a lace missing from his boot, visiting his shop some days after the murder and asking questions about it. After the trial was over the man was traced. He was a marine engineer from a Gorleston trawler who was at sea at the time of the crime.

The jury, faced with the choice of believing Mr Douglas or the impressive array of prosecution witnesses, did not take long to come to a decision. They were back after a delay of only thirty-five minutes with a verdict of 'Guilty'.

Herbert Bennett, throughout the seven-day trial, had appeared unbothered. He listened to all the evidence with interest but no apparent concern; he behaved as though it were not his life that was at stake; he smiled at those laboured jokes judges are so fond of. But he finally paled at the verdict, as if the outcome was entirely unexpected.

Herbert John Bennett then made a return journey to Norfolk and was hanged at Norwich on 21 March 1901.

During the trial Marshall Hall may, or may not, have impressed legal experts by his forensic skills, but he certainly did not impress the good people of Norfolk. As the *Yarmouth Independent* expressed it:

> ... he did not improve his case by traducing the character of Yarmouth in speaking of 'the prowling brutes who haunt the shore at Yarmouth'. We would advise Mr Marshall Hall not to venture a visit to our popular sea-side resort, for fear his presence should become known. The beachmen are up in arms against him, and if he should be seen 'prowling about the beach' his reception would be more demonstrative than polite. Yarmouth stands well with the public and such a base libel upon its fair fame is too bad, even in a counsel who has license to say anything he pleases, whether fact or fiction.

The 'great advocate' was no more popular in the Plumstead and Bexley Heath area where his deliberate bullying of decent, honest people like Mrs Elliston, whom he reduced to tears, was by no means well received.

It is the long-established convention in detective fiction that, in the last chapter when the great detective finally declares 'J'accuse,' the murderer not only confesses immediately but very helpfully explains the details of the case, thereby neatly tying-up all the loose ends. In the real world it is rarely like that. A confession only makes conviction more likely and it is human nature to go on hoping that 'something will turn up' long after there is the slightest chance that it will do so. Most murderers take their secrets with them to the grave and this was especially so when they were quickly hanged and there was little opportunity or incentive to sell their stories to the newspapers.

Bennett continued to declare himself innocent to the last, possibly because, by then, he had convinced himself that he was innocent. He was, as we have seen, an habitual liar, with a fondness for acting a part. Such men frequently delude themselves just as much as they delude others. The truth becomes not so much a matter of hard fact but rather what is convenient to believe.

That Bennett was indeed guilty is hardly a question for debate – the evidence was overwhelming. His motives are all too obvious. If he ever had loved his wife, by the time that they returned from South Africa he had clearly ceased to do so. She was an obvious impediment and a severe financial liability. He could hardly have enjoyed the situation in which, while Mary lived at Glencoe Villa, a pleasant if rather pretentiously named semi-detached house in Bexley Heath, he shared a room in a backstreet lodging-house in Woolwich. It was no doubt with a certain relish that he reversed this state of affairs in Yarmouth when he stayed in a hotel while Mary stayed in 'the Rows' with the Rudrums.

Had he been able simply to desert her he would, no doubt, have happily done so; but the possibility that she would divulge his secrets made that impracticable. When he then met Alice Meadows, younger and more attractive, the need for the removal of Mary developed a new urgency.

It has to be admitted that his plan for her murder was clever and very nearly succeeded. There was no reason to suppose that the body of Mrs Hood, on the beach at Yarmouth, would be connected with Mrs Bennett from Bexley Heath. After all, the only person likely to declare her missing was her husband and he, quite obviously, was not going to do so. By this time all contact between her and her parents seems to have ceased and he does not appear to have had much contact with his own.

Posting the letter from Woolwich was certainly a serious mistake and could have been easily avoided, but it was the laundry mark that really wrecked his carefully laid plans. The great weakness of his entire strategy was that it was based entirely upon a failure to identify the body. He had no 'fall-back position'. Once the police had discovered the connection with Mrs Bennett his entire defence effectively collapsed.

His immediate response of claiming not to recognize a photograph of his own wife, although others had already done so, destroyed him. It is easy to imagine the elation of Chief-Inspector Leach when he then searched Bennett's room and found the Yarmouth hotel receipt, together with the missing jewellery. If he were a drinking man he would have considered that worth a pint or two with his colleagues, especially given the number of laundries that they must have visited before finding the right one.

In some respects the tragedy of the Bennett family is a familiar story from fiction. A working-class young man, with a fondness for travel, for first-class tickets, for hotels, for ocean liners, is tied down with a wife and child. Unable to reconcile himself to his 'station in life', the normal life of a shop assistant and, becoming increasingly desperate to find some way out of the reality constantly closing in upon him, Bennett is fairly easy to understand.

Mary is an even more familiar figure. A young not very attractive girl marries far too soon, against parental advice, a handsome, charming man who turns out to be a less than perfect husband. For such a woman in 1900 there was little chance of escape, even without a child. Divorce was almost impossible and separation, without financial support, disastrous. There is, in any case, no evidence that she wished to get away from him, rather the reverse. So she hung on as best she could, using what weapons she possessed and continued to believe the stories he told her, including the one that took her to Yarmouth and her death.

The little blue-eyed, fair-haired Ruby, orphaned at the age of two, was adopted by Bennett's parents. After the trial a national newspaper launched an appeal on her behalf.

THE TEETOTAL
DRINKER

THE TEETOTAL DRINKER

In the early spring of 1900 Richard Brinkley faced a tricky problem. It was one that he had not foreseen and one to which he had to find a satisfactory solution, otherwise it could become disastrous for him. There was most certainly a large sum of money at stake and possibly his freedom as well. This very dangerous situation had arisen as the result of a carefully laid plan which had, initially, appeared to have been entirely successful. Now it was rapidly going very wrong indeed.

Brinkley, a fifty-three-year-old jobbing carpenter, lived at 42 Streatham Hill in a suburb of London south of the Thames. For a number of years he had been on friendly terms with an elderly lady, a Mrs Johanna Blume, of 4 Maxwell Road, Fulham. He visited her home regularly, spent a great deal of time chatting to her and was in the habit of calling her 'Granny'. For her part Mrs Blume enjoyed these little chats being, like many elderly people, rather lonely.

She seems to have had very few relatives, at any rate very few who took any real interest in her welfare. There were, however, two clear exceptions to this, these being her only daughter, Caroline Blume, and a grand-daughter, Caroline Granville. Both these two women visited her regularly and the old lady was known to be fond of them. As is usual in these matters, she was especially fond of her grand-daughter.

Another acquaintance of Richard Brinkley was Reginald Parker, an accountant employed in the City. The two men had known one another for some three or four years and, from time to time during this period, had organized small business deals together. These transactions usually involved the purchase and immediate resale, at a substantial profit, of dogs, cats and other domestic animals. Brinkley, who was rather good at cultivating people whom he thought might be of use to him, found Parker especially valuable. Not only did he have a knowledge of finance, which can often come in useful, but he could also be relied upon to assist Brinkley with any necessary writing. This was particularly helpful because the carpenter had great difficulty in spelling and was not 'a good penman', as they expressed it at the time.

Towards the end of 1899 Brinkley paid one of his occasional visits to Parker's home. He told his friend that he was intending to organize an outing and wished to collect the signatures of people interested in taking part. To enable him to do this he requested help in drawing-up a suitable form. Parker thereupon very helpfully drafted a simple form with rough details of the proposed outing at the top and spaces for prospective trippers to write their names and addresses below. Brinkley was clearly delighted with the result. It was, he said, just what he wanted.

Only a week or two later he once more approached Parker with a request for literary assistance. This time it involved preparing a sort of will. Amongst other items it referred to a Post Office savings-book and also to stocks and shares. The name Mrs Blume appeared. Brinkley told Parker that it was required for an elderly lady that he knew and who was particularly anxious to make a will. For this document, as for the outing-form, Parker used ordinary plain, foolscap paper.

Soon after these events Parker, who had been having personal problems for some time, finally parted from his wife and obtained lodgings for himself in Brixton. It was therefore to Brixton that Brinkley travelled on 19 December to once more visit his friend. After sitting talking for a while, they decided to go out for a drink together. While they were strolling along near Effra Road, Brinkley referred to the outing that he had mentioned on one of their previous meetings and asked Parker if he would like to come.

Parker, feeling a bit lonely and depressed now that he was separated from his wife, showed interest and his companion produced the familiar outing-form which Parker duly signed. A few minutes later, Brinkley asked him if he had signed both forms, explaining that he wanted to keep one of them for himself while distributing the other. The two men entered an ale-house where Parker enjoyed a very welcome glass of beer but Brinkley, who had 'signed the pledge', confined himself to lemonade. Parker, having admitted that he had only signed one copy of the outing-form, Brinkley produced from his pocket a sheet of paper that was folded over. His companion, now in a happier and more relaxed frame of mind with his friend and his beer, applied his name and address to it without bothering to open it out.

During the morning of that same day, 19 December, Mrs Blume's grand-daughter, Caroline Granville, made one of her frequent visits to the old lady. Caroline was an actress and, at the time, was busy rehearsing pantomime at the Fulham Empire. This was extremely convenient because it meant that she was able to see her grand-mother twice a day; a welcome respite from rehearsals. On this occasion the old lady was very cheerful and appeared to be in excellent health. And yet, within half an hour of Caroline leaving her, Mrs Blume was dead.

That evening when Caroline returned, expecting to have a meal and a pleasant talk with her grandmother, she found instead a solicitor searching for a will. She was unable to be of any assistance to him in that respect, but shortly afterwards Brinkley arrived. The solicitor asked him if he knew anything about the old lady's will and he, rather in the fashion of a conjurer producing a rabbit from a hat, took from his pocket a folded piece of paper which he declared to be Mrs Blume's will.

The will, which was dated only two days before, left everything to Richard Brinkley: her furniture, her household effects, her leasehold house, her stocks and shares, money in the Post Office – nothing had been forgotten. The total value was in the region of £800, a useful sum of money in 1899.

The witnesses to the will were shown as Reginald C. Parker of 60 Water Lane, Brixton and Henry J. Heard of 129 Hollydale Road, Peckham. The will had every indication of being genuine and was forwarded to Somerset House for registration. Mrs Blume's doctor decided that she had died of apoplexy and issued a certificate accordingly. Her funeral took place on a day of appalling winter weather, with rain falling continuously. Almost immediately Richard Brinkley moved into his newly acquired house in Maxwell Road. For him, everything had gone beautifully.

Now, it hardly needs to be said that the relatives of Mrs Blume, her daughter and grand-daughter in particular, were less than pleased by this sudden turn of events. They were indeed highly suspicious of the circumstances surrounding the old lady's death and less than convinced of the validity of the will. The necessary solicitor's advice was sought and quickly acted upon. The process of legally contesting the will began.

To Brinkley this was all very irritating. It was also extremely dangerous. It seems never to have occurred to him that it might be possible for the relatives legally to contest the will. It was very unfair, he had already declared to Miss Granville that he 'was now master of the house'. He had taken possession of the old lady's home and disposed of some of her personal property. Now it was all in doubt. Something had to be done to stop official enquiries. Then he had a brilliant idea.

He went to see Mrs Blume's daughter and told her that he did not need the money, he was really quite well off. What he actually wanted was to fulfil her mother's wishes and it had been her mother's dearest wish that they should marry. Much to his surprise she was not in the least enamoured by the suggestion. Indeed, she seemed to think it ridiculous; she said she couldn't even think of such a thing, he was a stranger. A day or two later, believing no doubt in the fickleness of women, he returned and proposed again. Once more she was unresponsive to his obvious charms and declined the wonderful opportunity he offered her. The behaviour of women really can be incomprehensible at times!

So now what? If lawyers and officials, perhaps even the police, started nosing around asking questions, what could they discover? They could not ask Mrs Blume if the will was genuine. She was safely dead and buried. Her signature on the will was no trouble: that was genuine. She just had not known what it was that she was signing. But what of the witnesses? Heard was not a problem. He had seen her sign the will all right, but he had assumed that she knew what she was doing.

No. There was only one real problem – Parker. If the police or someone went to Parker and asked him about the will that he had witnessed, he would say, 'What will? I haven't witnessed any will.' One thing was quite clear; somehow Parker had to be silenced, for good.

Brinkley knew that Parker had his own difficulties. He suffered from severe depression and a doctor had once warned his wife that he might try to kill himself. Suppose, just suppose, that Parker committed suicide? Yes. That would solve everything. Would be very neat and tidy.

One factor that was especially convenient for Brinkley's plans was that Parker was now living apart from his wife, although they were still on the friendliest of terms. Several times Brinkley invited his friend over to his new Fulham home but the offer was always, for one reason or another, declined. Since time was passing, bringing the legal investigation of the will nearer, this left Brinkley with no alternative but to try to achieve his objective at Parker's own home.

During March 1900, while Parker was living in Cobden Road, Norwood, he received visits from his carpenter friend on two successive evenings. On the first occasion Parker's brother was there preparing the evening meal. He offered some to Brinkley but it was politely declined with the explanation that he had only just had his tea. Upon learning that the brother would not be there the following night, however, Brinkley suggested that, if Parker would lend him his latch-key, he would come earlier the next day. He could then have the meal ready for Parker when he returned home, tired, from his work in the City. This very kind offer was refused.

At about a quarter past six the next evening Brinkley once more turned up at Cobden Road and, seeing that his host was busy writing a letter, offered to prepare the tea for him. Parker however, after remarking that the letter was not important and could easily wait, set about organizing the meal himself. While they were dining together, Brinkley suddenly acquired a cough and requested a glass of water. Parker, as a good host, went to the kitchen, leaving a partially drunk cup of tea on the table. Upon returning, he decided that the remaining tea was cold and chose not to drink it. This apparently insignificant series of events was to recur the following month with devastating results.

On 6 April Parker, feeling lonely living on his own, moved once again. He now obtained lodgings with Richard and Anne Beck who lived with their two daughters at 32 Churchill Road, Croydon. It was, and indeed still is, a solidly built Victorian semi-detached house in a quiet street off the Brighton Road. The Becks had lived there for about ten years. Richard Beck had at one time been a farmer but now, as a result of the severe depression in agriculture, made a living as a gardener. His two daughters were Daisy, aged twenty-one, who worked as a dressmaker and Hilda who was aged just nineteen.

Parker, not wanting to give embarrassing explanations, told Mr Beck that he was a single man. On one occasion when his wife came to visit him he introduced her to the Becks, not entirely inaccurately, as his lady-friend.

On Friday, 19 April, Parker received a letter from Brinkley telling him that he knew of someone who was looking for a good house-dog and asking if he knew where such an animal could be found. There would be a good profit in it. Parker, being an accountant, was never averse to a good profit and was soon making enquiries amongst the Croydon community. Given the strong incentive it did not take him long to find the ideal animal, a bull-dog owned by Mr John Marsh of 169 Brighton Road, only a short distance from Churchill Road.

He quickly despatched a postcard to Brinkley at Fulham informing him of his success. At about midday on Saturday his associate telephoned him and asked him to deliver the dog to Fulham that same afternoon. Parker told him that that was quite impossible, it simply could not be done. After further discussion, it was arranged that Brinkley would come over to Croydon that evening between seven and eight o'clock to inspect the animal.

Soon after seven o'clock that evening Parker collected the bull-dog from John Marsh, telling him that he was going to show it to a potential buyer. He took it to Churchill Road where it was seen and admired by Daisy Beck.

Early that evening, nineteen-year-old Hilda Beck left the house with her mother and, at about 8.15 p.m., Daisy went out to meet her young man, Alfred Young. This meant that the only people left in the house were Parker and Mr Beck who produced two bottles of Fremlins Ale. The two men sat talking for a while, drinking, during which time they succeeded in emptying one of the bottles. Then Mr Beck left the house, leaving Parker alone and waiting for his expected visitor.

Meanwhile, Brinkley left Maxwell Road. Henry Dame of Basuto Road, Parsons Green, an inspector with the West London Extension Railway, was on duty that evening at Chelsea Station near Stamford Bridge football ground. This was only a few hundred yards from Maxwell Road. At about six o'clock he saw Brinkley, whom he had known for some years, walk along the down platform and cross the footbridge onto the up side. He was well in time to catch the 6.15 p.m. train to Clapham Junction where a connecting train took him to Croydon which he reached by 7.20 p.m.

Leaving the station he made his way to the Brighton Road and began the longish walk to Churchill Road. It was not only a long walk, it was also a rather lonely one. There had been a time when the Brighton Road had seen a constant stream of stage coaches and private carriages, plus numerous riders on horseback and even herds of animals, all making their way to or from the fashionable Regency resort. There would likewise come a time when it would once more be packed with traffic, cars lined bumper to bumper as far as the eye could see, all heading for the coast. But Brinkley was walking during 'the age of the train'. The only traffic comprised local tradesmen's carts, together with cabs and private carriages bearing their passengers only as far as the nearest railway station. Once clear of the towns the Brighton Road was empty with tufts of grass and dandelions growing in the middle.

At 149 Brighton Road, about midway between South Croydon Station and Churchill Road, there was a corner beer-shop which still survives to this day as an off-licence. At that time it was in the hands of a Mrs Hardstone. On the evening in question, in addition to herself, there was present a customer, George Titmus, and a thirteen-year-old boy, John Holden, who helped in the shop.

At around about 7.30 p.m. Brinkley entered the tiny room which served both as a shop and a bar. He requested a bottle of Oatmeal Stout to 'take away'. Mrs Hardstone lifted a bottle off the shelf and asked him how far he was taking it. He replied, 'Just around the corner.' Mrs Hardstone then carefully rubber-stamped the bottle with the shop's name and address and asked the customer for a deposit of 2d on the bottle. For some reason Brinkley took great exception to this perfectly normal request, there was an argument and he walked out without the stout. Some twenty minutes later he once more entered the little shop, again asked for a bottle of Oatmeal Stout, was asked for 2d on the bottle and paid it without comment.

When, shortly afterwards, Brinkley arrived at 32 Churchill Road Parker let him in and led the way into the sitting-room. Standing on the table were two bottles of Fremlins Ale, one of which was already empty, the other unopened. Brinkley produced the bottle of stout from his pocket and suggested that Parker might care to join him. When Parker, who knew his companion to be a teetotaller, expressed surprise, Brinkley explained that he had no choice in the matter, it was 'doctor's orders'.

The bottle was therefore opened and part of the contents poured into two glasses. The two men then sat discussing the proposed sale and resale of the dog, sipping their stout as they did so. After a while, Brinkley had one of his outbreaks of coughing and asked for a glass of water. Just as he had done in his previous home, Parker went into the kitchen to fetch it. In a short time he returned with the water, some of which his companion drank. This seemed to be effective because Brinkley ceased to cough.

By now complete agreement had been reached about the dog. Brinkley would buy it for £5 and Parker would take it over to Fulham the next morning. Brinkley would not take it himself because, he said, he was afraid that it might bite him. Both men now left the house. They walked a short distance together and then parted, Brinkley saying that he had to meet someone at Thornton Heath while Parker set off to return the dog to John Marsh and inform him of the successful sale.

While Parker was away from the house the Beck family was beginning to return. At about 10.45 p.m. Daisy and her mother both returned to find the house empty. Daisy soon went out again for a short time to say goodnight to her young man at the back-gate. At about eleven o'clock Mr Beck returned with Hilda. Shortly after eleven Parker once more entered the house. He sat down with Mr Beck at the sitting-room table and told him about the plan to deliver the dog to Fulham the next day. It was now intended to convey it in John Marsh's pony and trap and, in order to ensure an early start, he would spend the night with Mr Marsh. As the two men talked, they opened and drank the second bottle of Fremlins Ale.

Parker made his departure at 11.35 p.m. and the Beck household began to settle down for the night. Hilda, the youngest girl, soon went off to bed. Mr and Mrs Beck remained at the sitting-room table. Mr Beck reached out for the bottle of stout and divided the contents between two glasses. He and his wife each drank some. Daisy had a sip from her mother's glass but said that she didn't like it, it was too bitter.

Mrs Beck rose to her feet and walked into the kitchen. Almost immediately there was a choking noise and then the sound of a heavy fall. Her husband quickly went to find out what had happened to her and a moment later was calling for assistance. Now it was the turn of Daisy Beck to go into the kitchen. She discovered her mother stretched out on the floor groaning, her father bending over her. Only a few seconds later she felt as if she, herself, was suffocating and fell to the floor, unconscious.

Her sister Hilda was already in bed, but luckily not asleep, when her father called out to her for help. Slipping on a dressing-gown she went rapidly downstairs and through into the sitting-room. She found her mother sitting in an armchair, groaning and making horrible choking noises. Her father knelt by her mother's side. Stretched out on a couch nearby lay her sister, apparently unconscious.

Mr Beck hammered urgently on the wall and they both shouted for help from their neighbours at number 34. Mr and Mrs Collinson responded quickly and came in to assist. Upon discovering the serious nature of the emergency Mrs Collinson went out again to call a doctor and to fetch a bottle of brandy from her own house, leaving her husband behind with the Beck family. Hardly had she left the house when Mr Beck also collapsed and began making the same choking noises as his wife, as if he were suffocating.

When, in response to the urgent call from Mrs Collinson, Dr Dempster arrived upon the scene he found Mr and Mrs Beck clearly dying, their elder daughter unconscious. Within only a few minutes of his arrival, both the parents were dead. For Daisy there was still some hope and he had her rushed to Croydon Hospital.

The doctor then turned his attention to the dazed and desperately upset Hilda, anxious to know precisely how such a tragedy could have occurred. She told him that when she went to bed all three had been sitting at the table, healthy and happy. Dr Dempster then examined the three beer bottles still standing on the sitting-room table. When he picked up and cautiously smelt the stout bottle it had the unmistakable smell of potassium cyanide. He immediately sent for the police.

The arrival of the police was followed almost immediately by the police surgeon, Dr George Genge. Their examination of the stout bottle, together with judicious questioning of the greatly shocked Hilda and of the Collinsons, soon led the police to John Marsh's home in the Brighton Road. It still being very early in the morning it took a little time to rouse the occupants. Reginald Parker was informed that there had been a tragedy at the Beck house but its precise nature was not divulged. He was then conveyed to the local police station and subjected to a thorough interrogation. He was, after all, the obvious suspect. He lived with the victims, had been with them only a short time before, was most probably the provider of the deadly stout and had made an excuse to leave the house shortly before the disaster.

His story was, however, entirely plausible. He impressed the experienced police officers by his manner and his evident ignorance of the fate of his hosts; many of the facts he gave could easily be checked. That the poisoned stout bottle carried a supplier's name and address was of considerable assistance; such a bottle could have been purchased at any one of thousands of public-houses and ale-shops in the city with no means of identification.

It did not take the police long to interview Mrs Hardstone and then her young assistant, John Holden. They soon had confirmation of at least part of Parker's story. He was most definitely not the man who had purchased the bottle of Oatmeal Stout and young Holden gave them a good description of the man who had. A description which tallied exactly with that given by Parker of his friend Brinkley.

By now Daisy Beck, though still in hospital, was beginning to recover. Luckily she had drunk only a small sip of the stout. It was, however, a clear indication of how much poison had been added to the bottle to make it so very deadly.

Throughout Sunday the police continued their enquiries and gradually became more and more certain of the crime's perpetrator. Late that same evening, just as it was becoming dark, Detective-Inspector Fowler, accompanied by Sergeant Easter, mounted a watch upon 4 Maxwell Road. The two policemen had a long wait because it was not until shortly before midnight that a man answering Brinkley's description was seen walking leisurely down the street towards the house. The police officers shrank back into the shadows and waited until the man mounted the steps of number 4, and was already fiddling with keys, before they acted. Stepping out into the light from an adjacent gas-lamp, they blocked his possible escape-route. Detective-Inspector Fowler, showing his warrant-card, said,

'We are police officers and I shall arrest you for administering poison in a bottle of stout to Reginald Parker at Croydon last night, with intent to murder him.'

'Well, I'm sugared,' was Brinkley's response.

D.I. Fowler then formally cautioned him, to which Brinkley commented that he had not been anywhere near Croydon that night. Told that he would most probably be charged with the murder of Mr and Mrs Beck, who had both died as a result of the poison, he said:

'Well, I'm sugared. This is very awkward, is it not?'

He was informed that he would be taken to Fulham Police Station. On the way there he remarked that he had not seen Parker for three weeks. Later, as he was being placed in a cell at the police station, he asked, with some surprise:

'You are not going to keep me all night, are you?'

Told that this was very much their intention, he complained:

'This is Parker playing a trick on me, he is a dirty tyke.'

At five o'clock on the Monday morning he was taken from his cell, placed in a police-van and so began the journey back to Croydon. Soon after leaving Fulham, Brinkley asked his escort:

'Does Parker say I done it? They won't believe him. He is a dirty b— tyke and spiteful towards everyone if they speak to his wife. His mother and wife are beautiful people, they won't have him. If anyone says I bought beer, they have got to prove it. I am a good character and a teetotaller.'

At no point had anyone said anything to him about buying beer.

Later that same morning, Brinkley was placed in a line with nine other men at Croydon Police Station. The three people from the Brighton Road beer-shop were brought in one at a time and asked if they could identify the purchaser of the Oatmeal Stout. Mrs Hardstone was first, but was unable to identify anyone. Next came George Titmus. He identified Brinkley, saying that, when seen in the shop, his moustache had been different, darker and curled. In spite of that difference he had no doubt whatever that it was the same man. Thirteen-year-old John Holden, when brought before the parade of men, looked along the line and immediately walked straight up to Brinkley.

As police investigations continued, new evidence emerged. A thorough search of Brinkley's belongings brought to light some interesting and curious documents. One was an exact, word-perfect copy of Mrs Blume's will but with an entirely false name and address. With it was another document in which the first two lines and the bottom lines were once again identical to the will. In this case, however, the centre section of the paper bore the words 'hearby declare myself to be a visitor of Mr Brinkley to the Annual Ladies Ball, and also my niece, Augusta Granville'. Each of these documents was in Brinkley's handwriting.

In view of the obvious implications of these papers and of the serious nature of the charges which Brinkley was already facing, an order was obtained for the exhumation of the body of Mrs Blume. Possibly due to the delay in carrying out a thorough examination, coupled with the limitations of the techniques then available, the results of the long overdue post-mortem were inconclusive. Meanwhile, a post-mortem examination of the bodies of Mr and Mrs Beck had come up with the answer that everyone was expecting. Both bodies contained large quantities of potassium cyanide as did the two glasses.

The police now learnt of a curious incident that had taken place on the Sunday morning, the day after the murders. At about 7.10 a.m. Brinkley went to a newspaper shop in Fulham, run by a Mr Hayward, and used the public callbox there. The recipient of the call was a Miss Susan White who lived in Brighton Road, not far from

John Marsh. The caller asked for Parker. John Marsh was called to the phone and said that Parker was not there, but did not say where he was. At that time Parker was still being grilled at the police station. The caller, who said that his name was Brinkley, asked that a message be passed to Parker. It was that Parker should not take the dog to Fulham that morning as it was too fierce, but that he should come himself that evening.

Investigations further afield produced evidence from a Mr William Vale. Mr Vale was a veterinary surgeon specializing in the diseases of birds. He did not, however, confine himself entirely to birds but also treated other creatures, including dogs and cats. He had known Brinkley for fourteen years and in June 1899 had engaged him to do some carpentry work in his house. During a conversation with him there, Brinkley asked him for some prussic acid to poison a dog, a practice by no means uncommon in those days. Mr Vale gave him a little, about sixty drops. A few days later Brinkley requested some more, saying that he had accidentally spilt the original dose. Mr Vale once more complied with his request, another sixty drops. As he did so, Brinkley was in the perfect position to see precisely where the drugs were kept, in an unlocked cupboard, and also which was the correct bottle. After that he visited the house another three or four times, with ample opportunity to help himself to further poison.

The eventual trial of Richard Brinkley, at the Surrey County Assizes, was held at Guildford in July and opened to the dramatic accompaniment of a violent and spectacular thunderstorm.

Defence counsel tried to support his contention that the defendant had not been to Croydon on the night of the murders. To stand any chance whatever in this task he needed, first of all, totally to discredit Reginald Parker. He endeavoured to do this by several means. Much was made of his medical condition, it being suggested that, because he suffered from depression, he might also suffer from delusions. His doctor would have none of it and no other doctor was produced by the defence to support such an unlikely theory. Attempts were made to question his honesty, again with little success. The fact that he was living apart from his wife was made much of. But, in truth, even if defence counsel had succeeded in casting doubt in the minds of the jury as to the reliability of Parker's evidence they still had to deal with all the other witnesses.

This was no easy task, for none of them had any conceivable motive for committing perjury. Counsel tried very hard to argue that, since Mrs Hardstone had not been able to identify Brinkley, the other two occupants of the shop, George Titmus and John Holden, must be mistaken. But this was a form of logic that the rest of the court found difficulty in following.

What of the strange telephone call received by Susan White and John Marsh? This they said was from a man called Brinkley and involved a bull-dog being taken to Fulham. How on earth could they possibly have invented such a story? Susan White had no reason to know that such a person as Brinkley even existed, let alone that he was negotiating to purchase a bull-dog. Once again the defence could only airily dismiss the evidence by declaring that the witnesses were mistaken.

In a similar fashion, defence counsel suggested that Henry Dame was simply wrong when he claimed to have seen the defendant walk along the platform of Chelsea Station on the evening of the murders. But Dame had known Brinkley for a number of years and railway inspectors can normally be relied upon to have their wits about them.

For his part, Brinkley claimed that he spent the night in question with friends. If that was the case, why did defence counsel not call these friends to the witness-box? Brinkley also claimed that Heard could testify that Johanna Blume's will was perfectly correct. But, once again, the witness was not called to give his valuable evidence.

While Parker was able to bring a steady stream of witnesses to support his side of the argument, Brinkley failed to produce a single one to support his. Given this completely one-sided balance of the evidence, the resulting verdict was a foregone conclusion. Guilty.

The opinion of the people of Croydon about the case and its outcome was expressed by the *Croydon Advertiser*, in its own peculiar style, in its edition of 17 August.

There is no occasion to disown any unworthy feeling when we express a satisfaction which will be generally shared throughout Croydon that events have put an end to the unpleasant notoriety in which Croydon found itself in the early spring – a spring, by the way, which was forestalled and apparently abolished by a too early appearance of Easter, and has since given place to a summer which is scarcely more than a name. Brinkley's execution on Tuesday has put an end, let us hope, to the discussions that have taken place in all quarters on what is known as the Croydon poisoning case, and other circumstances have helped to put an end to the unsavoury comment on other subjects not pleasant to the people of Croydon. Though not very stern advocates of capital punishment, we do not think that there is likely to be any great feeling of regret of the fate that has overtaken Brinkley. Truly the world is rid of a miserable man.

The question that needs to be asked about the Brinkley case is not whether he was guilty of the murder of Mr and Mrs Beck. Of that there has never been any doubt. No. The real question is whether his plan could have worked? Did he really stand any chance of murdering Reginald Parker and getting away with it?

It does not seem likely. Supposing that everything had gone according to plan. Parker would have returned to the house after parting from Brinkley, drunk the poisoned stout and died. What would have happened? Brinkley, of course, believed that everyone would say, 'Poor Parker has committed suicide,' and then forget all about it. But that is just wishful thinking.

Let us look first at the way he would have died. Is it usual for a man to kill himself by adding potassium cyanide to the contents of a bottle of stout and then pouring the poisoned stout into a glass before drinking it? Why not just drink the cyanide? Or, if he insisted on mixing it with stout, surely the obvious thing to do is to pour the stout into a glass and then add the poison.

Secondly, there is the question of Parker's visitor. A number of people knew that he was expecting someone. The bull-dog ensured that. The Becks almost certainly knew. John Marsh must have known. The presence of the bottle of stout, which had been poured into two glasses, also indicated a visitor. Why would Parker go out to buy a bottle of stout when there was already a bottle of ale standing unopened on the sitting-room table?

The answer, of course, is that Brinkley made the same mistake as he had made with Mrs Blume's will. Just as he believed that no one would question the validity of the will, so he now believed that no one would question Parker's apparent suicide. In reality the police would be bound to make enquiries. Pure routine. And the incident would not stand up to even a minimum investigation.

The curiosity of the police once aroused, where would they go? To the beer-shop, whose name and address was so conveniently on the bottle. His behaviour in the shop ensured that he would be remembered. To get into an argument over paying 2d on the bottle, when he was intending to employ that same bottle to commit a murder, was an act of almost unbelievable stupidity.

Once having established that Parker did not buy the stout himself, the police would have confirmation that there had, indeed, been a visitor. Next, they would need to establish his identity. That could have been done easily enough. Parker's wife could tell them. She knew of his association with Brinkley and of their trading in animals. Given the presence of the dog, together with the story told to John Marsh, the most likely identity of the mysterious visitor was Richard Brinkley. If the appearance of Brinkley then tallied with that of the beer-shop customer, the police would be well on their way to an arrest.

The strangest thing about Brinkley's behaviour was that he left so much to chance, something was almost bound to go wrong. The purchase of the stout, for instance. Having gone to so much trouble to acquire the cyanide and in planning for its use, why did he give so little thought to the drink that he would add it to? When he left Fulham did he really have no idea of how he was going to administer it? Did he only have the idea of a bottle of stout when, during his long walk from the station, he came upon a beer-shop? Surely, if he had planned all along to use a bottle of stout, he would have obtained one elsewhere in London and brought it with him?

How could he be sure that, when he reached Churchill Road, he would find Parker alone? The answer is that he could have no idea whether the Beck family would be there or not. The fact that Parker was alone when he arrived was pure luck. It was perhaps this lucky chance for Brinkley that led him to be so sloppy in the use of the cyanide. Because the Beck family were not there, he forgot all about them. It never entered his head that they might return and consume the poisoned drink. His total lack of foresight led first to the deaths of Mr and Mrs Beck and then inevitably to his own.

THE GROCER'S
ASSISTANT

THE GROCER'S ASSISTANT

It was late in the afternoon of 23 December 1902. Church Road, Leyton, was busy with the clip-clop of horses' hooves and the clatter of cartwheels. Men and women moved hurriedly to and fro, eager to get to their homes and their dinners, for it was already becoming dark.

Suddenly, from what appeared to be the closed and empty shop at number 89, there came the sound of breaking glass, frantic cries for help and the bangs and crashes of a violent fight. Two carmen, Robert Smith and Herbert Pitt, hearing the commotion, left their tram and, joined by a dustman, George Wheatly, converged on the shop, keen to discover precisely what was happening and ready to offer assistance.

At that time Leyton was in the front line of London's headlong expansion, Church Road being still semi-rural. Number 89 was the end house of a short terrace of only four houses and was, in itself, no different from thousands more: a small shop on the ground floor, with living accommodation above. At the rear there were small gardens and, beyond the terrace, a coalyard which still showed signs of having once been a farmyard. Across the street were open fields stretching to Hackney Marshes, dank and dreary on a December afternoon.

As the three men approached the house the door burst open, a man staggered out and collapsed on the pavement, covered in blood. His assailant, who had begun to follow the injured man, saw the newcomers, changed his mind and retreated into the darkness of the building.

George Wheatly quickly ran round the back of the house and saw a man washing his hands in an old bath which stood in the garden. Wheatly picked up a brick and when the man prepared to escape by climbing over the garden wall he blocked his way, threatening him with the brick and saying, 'You've nearly killed that man and now I'll kill you.' The man, faced by such a determined adversary, backed away and once more returned to the house.

When Constable Matthews arrived on the scene he found the victim, somewhat recovered but still dazed and bleeding from a head-wound, sitting on the pavement outside the shop and surrounded by sympathetic helpers. The broken door of the house stood wide open and there was neither sight nor sound within.

Leaving the front door well guarded P.C. Matthews, taking Robert Smith with him, made his way through the next-door house, number 91, into the back garden of number 89 and thence into the house. Finding no sign of life on the ground floor they went, with understandable caution, up the stairs and onto the landing. The two men now found themselves facing a bedroom door, locked on the inside. Constable Matthews hammered on the door in his best professional 'name of the law' manner, but without obtaining any response from within. They thereupon put their shoulders to work and smashed it open.

A man was sitting on the bed in the process of calmly changing his blood-stained shirt. When told that he was being arrested he said, 'I was assaulted first and picked up the first thing I could lay my hands on to strike him with.' Giving his name as Edgar Edwards and his occupation as grocer's assistant, he was taken to Stratford Police Station. When formally charged with assault, his reply was, 'I am very sorry it occurred. We had been drinking together.'

The injured man, now identified as John Garland, a grocer of Godrell Road, Victoria Park, had meanwhile been taken to West Ham Hospital. He was detained there for a week with head injuries.

In their investigations of the incident the police were soon faced with two accounts that bore almost no resemblance to one another. First, there was Edwards, a thirty-four-year-old man with a receding forehead and piercing steel-blue eyes above a small fair moustache and a receding chin.

According to him, it was all very simple. He and Garland had been out drinking together. No doubt partly as a result of the alcohol, they had quarrelled and the quarrel had turned violent, as such quarrels often do. Garland had attacked him and he had defended himself as best as he could. It was a plausible enough story, the police heard similar stories every week, apart from the curious fact that, while Garland had suffered serious head injuries, Edwards appeared to have suffered virtually no injuries at all.

When the police were able to obtain a full statement from Garland, however, they heard a completely different story. He was a strongly built man and with his quiet, humorous, self-reliant manner, his dark skin and square jaw, together with a full moustache drooping over a firm mouth, looked very much like a retired non-commissioned officer.

Garland and his wife had a small grocer's shop in Victoria Park and, wishing to sell it, they approached a reputable business agency, Duggan & Co. of Bishopsgate. Duggan, in turn, then advertised the business in the usual way.

On 18 December Edwards came to the shop and showed them an 'order to view' from the agency. He was invited in and shown over the premises; he expressed great interest in the fact that there was a side door which he said would be very useful. He was allowed to inspect the books and commented that they seemed to do quite a lot of business. In response to questions, Garland explained that he and his wife managed the shop entirely on their own. This aspect of the business seemed greatly to impress the prospective buyer.

In due course, the inevitable question of price arose and Garland said that he was asking £80, the amount stated in the agency advertisement. Edwards appeared to be perfectly happy with that and suggested that they went to Duggan & Co. immediately, but then realized that it was too late in the day. He left soon afterwards, saying that he would write and arrange an appointment to finalize the sale.

A few days later, on 22 December, Garland received a letter from Edwards:

> As I shall be at Leyton tomorrow, could you make it convenient to meet me at eleven o'clock at 89 Church Rd, Leyton to talk over matters, and accompany me to Duggans in order to make the necessary arrangements and pay a substantial deposit.

Unfortunately, Garland did not receive the letter until 11.30 a.m. on the day of the proposed meeting and was quite obviously unable to keep the suggested appointment. He therefore went to Duggan's office in Bishopsgate, told them of the developing situation and then sent a telegram to the address on Edwards's letter, 5 Barnsbury Road, Islington, explaining his failure to put in an appearance. The following day he received another letter from Edwards:

Waited about at Leyton until past one o'clock. Saw nothing of you. Must be there again tomorrow and if you can possibly make it convenient to see me at 89 Church Rd between eleven and twelve, I should be greatly obliged. The facts are these. I have just let the house, and the tenant wants to come in on Wednesday and there are some repairs which require my superintendence. Hoping you can see me there tomorrow, as I have so much on my hands just now.

Accordingly, Garland made his way to Leyton and by eleven o'clock had found the empty shop in Church Road. He was admitted to the house by Edwards who said that he was awaiting the arrival of a carpenter who was coming from one of his other properties, a house at Clapton. The man had a small amount of work to finish there but that should not take him more than an hour and he would then come to Leyton to attend to the required repairs in the Church Road premises. So far as Garland could tell, the building was completely empty; certainly there was no sign of furniture on the ground floor. While they were talking, Edwards held in his right hand what appeared to be a roll of paper; this Garland assumed to be drawings of the house.

They had a lengthy discussion about the Victoria Park business, during the course of which Edwards asked Garland:

'Would you mind after I have taken the business coming in for a few days to see how I get on?'

To which request, Garland replied that he would be quite prepared to do so, although only for a week.

Negotiations having been concluded to their mutual satisfaction, they left the shop and walked the hundred yards or so to the Oliver Twist public-house where they each had two glasses of ale. Edwards asked the landlord for a railway timetable and, having been given one, began to study it carefully, saying that they would go together to Liverpool Street and thence to the office of Duggan & Co. where they could finalize the matter and he would hand over the required deposit.

Unfortunately, this could not be done until the arrival of the elusive carpenter so they once more returned to the house to await him. Edwards explained that the house belonged to him but that it had been empty for about three months. A very good new tenant had now been found who was especially anxious to move in the next day.

But still the carpenter failed to put in an appearance for which Edwards continued to apologize, saying that he couldn't understand what on earth was causing the delay and assuring Garland that the man was bound to arrive at any moment. Having time to waste, they went out into the back garden together; Edwards pointed out that it had all been recently dug in readiness for the new tenant.

After continuing to hang about for some time, they went again to the Oliver Twist, had some more drinks and Edwards once more studied the railway timetable. At about three o'clock they returned to the house and once more stood around chatting, waiting for the still absent carpenter.

Garland, by now growing increasingly bored and impatient, and beginning to doubt whether the carpenter would ever turn up, declared that he really must get back to Victoria Park, never having intended being away so long. Edwards asked him whom he had left in charge and was told, 'Only my wife.' In response to further questioning, Garland once more assured Edwards that no one else was employed in the shop, not even a boy.

Shortly after this, Garland finally lost patience, commented that it was beginning to get dark and that even if the carpenter did materialize it was already too late to go to Bishopsgate. He declared his intention of leaving. Edwards did not argue but produced a pencil and a piece of paper, saying that he would write his instructions for the carpenter and leave them for him.

The two men then began to leave the shop, going first into the dark passage leading to the street door, Garland in the lead. Just as he was reaching to open the front door he received a violent blow on the back of his head, quickly followed by another. Being taken totally by surprise by the sudden unprovoked onslaught, he fell to the floor and lay there, desperately trying to protect his head with his arm while Edwards stood over him, raining blows upon him with what appeared to be the roll of paper.

With the desperate strength of a man knowing his life to be at stake, Garland somehow succeeded in getting back onto his feet, despite the seemingly endless blows directed upon him. There then took place a bitter struggle, during the course of which Edwards tried to silence Garland's cries for help by forcing a piece of cloth or handkerchief into his mouth. Garland gasped, 'Don't murder me - what have I done?' But still the attack continued until, with a final effort, Garland managed to reach the street door, smash one of the glass panels and call for help. A moment later the door burst open, Garland fell out onto the pavement and knew no more until he came round with Robert Smith and the other men bending over him.

So what was the truth of the matter? Was it, as Edwards argued, just a drunken quarrel that got out of hand? Or was it an entirely unprovoked attack with murderous intent, as claimed by Garland? And if it was attempted murder, what was the motive? Why should a man, who has amicably spent most of the day with another, suddenly decide to kill him?

It was in search of answers to these questions that the police went back to the closed shop in Church Road. Detective-Inspector Collins and Inspector Young let themselves into the house and began carefully to explore. The ground floor was just as Garland had told them, completely unfurnished. In the passage were blood-stains on the floor and walls. In the scullery were marks of blood on the fastenings of both door and window. On the floor they found a 5lb weight designed for a sash window, together with a roll of paper. Both items were blood-stained and had what appeared to be human hair still adhering to them. In the back garden was a bath containing red-coloured water. Making their way upstairs they soon found a washbasin containing similar, blood-stained water and, in a back room, a white shirt and vest covered in blood.

In their exploration of the upper floor they also discovered more intriguing items: business cards and pawn-tickets bearing the name of W.J. Darby and the address of 22 Wyndham Road, Camberwell. Their enquiries had already revealed that Edwards lived alone in the house. Were Edwards and Darby the same man? And why were there items of women's clothing in the house?

At their request, Detective-Sergeant Melville of Camberwell went to Wyndham Road to make enquiries about the mysterious W.J. Darby. What he learned caused them great concern.

Number 22 Wyndham Road, just off the busy Camberwell Road, was very similar to 89 Church Road, a small shop with living accommodation above. But what was really disturbing was the story told by the local people. They related that, until recently, the shop had been a grocers, run by a Mr and Mrs Darby, a friendly young couple who had lived there with their three-month-old child.

On the morning of 1 December a local baker, named Newby, had delivered bread to the shop at 8.45 a.m. and spoke to Mr Darby. At about eleven o'clock a Mr Whittington also went into the shop and had a conversation with Mr Darby who seemed perfectly normal. At one o'clock, however, when a customer went to the shop she was surprised to find it shut and when she returned at five she discovered, to her astonishment, that the Darbys had gone and the shop was now apparently in the possession of a hunch-backed man called Goodwin. He told her that he had taken over the management. The local people learned subsequently that Goodwin was, in fact, acting for a man called Edwards.

The Camberwell police were also told that a sister of Mrs Darby, a Mrs Alice Baldwin of Catford, had been to the shop asking for her sister, without success. D.S. Melville obtained entry to the shop from the landlord. At various places on the floor were blood-stains, some of which showed signs of attempts having been made to remove them. He also found a 5lb sash-weight, remarkably similar to the one found at Leyton. This one also bore traces of blood and human hair.

As a result of this disturbing new evidence, the police sent a telegram to Mrs Baldwin asking her to come to Stratford, which she soon did. The story that she had to tell was that her sister Beatrice, aged twenty-eight, a bright, happy young woman, had married William Darby about two years before. He was the son of a widow who kept a coffee-shop in Trafalgar Road, Greenwich. The marriage was obviously a happy one and had been crowned when their little girl, Ethel, was born in October.

After their marriage they set up in business running a china shop in High Road, Leytonstone and had then moved to Camberwell about eight months ago. That area of Camberwell was, however, an extremely poor one, with the result that the new business failed to prosper. When Mrs Baldwin had last spoken to them they were seriously considering selling it.

On 3 December Mrs Baldwin travelled to Camberwell to visit her sister whom she had last seen in the middle of November. Much to her surprise, when she entered the shop she found behind the counter not her sister or brother-in-law but a complete stranger, a man with a hunch-back who told her that he was now managing the shop. After about half an hour, during which time she had tried and failed to discover where the Darbys had gone, another man entered the shop. He told her that his name was Edwards and that he had purchased the business from the Darbys for £50. In reply to further questions, she was informed that the Darbys were staying with friends and that their furniture was 'locked up'.

She was, however, told that William Darby was expected at any moment and that he would be able to explain more fully. Mrs Baldwin thereupon declared her intention of waiting to see her brother-in-law. Time passed without any sign of him. Edwards expressed surprise at the delay and assured her that he would not be long. Finally, at 8.45 p.m., Mrs Baldwin could wait no longer and prepared to leave. As she made her departure Edwards commented, 'It is strange he doesn't come, he was here last night.'

After telling the police her story, Alice Baldwin was taken to visit the shop in nearby Church Road, Leyton. Once there, she was shown into the upstairs room and asked if she could recognize anything belonging to the Darby family. Her response was immediate:

'Why, that's her wedding dress! And this is their furniture and that is her new coat. Why, she only had one coat. What has become of her? How could she go without it?'

The police gave no reply to her questions but their thoughts went to the back of the house and the newly dug garden.

Following their interview with Mrs Baldwin and the obviously serious turn that the case had now taken, the police held a conference at Stratford. Detective-Inspector Collins, Inspector Young, Detective-Sergeant Melville and other experienced officers took part. They discussed the evidence already obtained and considered their future course of action.

The next morning three of their men, D.S. Melville, D.S. Friend and P.C. Hughes were sent to dig up the garden of the Leyton shop. The task given to them was both difficult and unpleasant. The whole of the garden had been well dug over and thoroughly manured, with the result that there was no indication whatever as to where any bodies or other evidence might have been buried. They had no alternative but systematically to dig it all.

The three men set to work. After several hours of arduous and unsuccessful labour they came across an area where the lower soil was a great deal looser, indicating recent disturbance. They dug steadily down into the soft earth with a mixture of anticipation and dread. At last, nearly five feet down, they came upon six sacks and a bundle. These they carried, somewhat gingerly, for their contents were all too obvious, into the house to await examination by the police surgeon who bore the interesting name of Dr Jekyll.

The contents of the sacks were horrific. They contained the remains of a man and a woman. Both bodies had been skilfully dismembered, heads and limbs severed, the joints carefully sawn. The pieces had then been bundled indiscriminately into the sacks, male and female mixed together. The body of little three-month-old Ethel was intact, but she still had a handkerchief tied tightly round her tiny throat.

On the first day of 1903, Stratford Police Court was witness to a scene whose quiet ordinariness only increased the drama. It took place in a lobby where twelve men brought in from the street stood in a line. Then another man entered, escorted by a strong police guard. To the casual eye he appeared no different to any other man in his round felt hat and winter overcoat. He had an air of total unconcern, almost indifference. An inspector told him to join the line of men. 'Stand where you like in the row,' he said, and Edwards did so.

A procession of witnesses came and went. All were asked the same question, 'Do you see anyone you know?' Almost all, in their markedly different ways, gave the same answer.

'That man,' said one, touching him on the shoulder.

'I know that man,' said a little hunch-back man.

'That is the man,' said the sister of the murdered woman.

There was drama of a different kind when Edwards was taken before the Stratford magistrates. A large and angry crowd massed before the court entrance as the police forced a way through. When, after the short hearing he once more emerged, the crowd was even larger and angrier, the booing and jeering rising to a crescendo as the prison van containing him passed slowly and with some difficulty through their ranks.

Police enquiries were, meanwhile, continuing and produced new witnesses and new evidence. This enabled them gradually to build up a picture of Edwards's movements and actions over the previous four or five weeks.

On 26 November he had called on Sarah Summers, a middle-aged woman living in Hampstead. Some thirteen years before she had had a child by him but had neither seen nor heard from him for some time. He told her that he had just bought a shop, the previous owner having died. He explained to her that, in addition to the business, the building also included living accommodation and, as he had purchased the furniture as well as the business, he was now in a position to provide a home for her. She could look after the shop for him and live on the premises.

A couple of days later, on the morning of the 28th, he called again and offered to take her to the shop that same evening. She could then have a good look around and see if it suited her. He did warn her, however, that there was one room that she would not be able to see. Having raised her expectations as well as her curiosity, he then failed to keep the appointment. Instead, he simply sent her a telegram saying that he had changed his mind. He gave no further explanation and she never saw him again.

That very same afternoon, Edwards turned up at the home of Mr and Mrs Goodwin who lived in Elsted Street, Walworth, not far from the Wyndham Road shop. Mr Goodwin, who was a hunch-back, had known Edwards for a very long time. They had attended the same school, Fellows Street School in Hackney Road, and had also gone to the same Sunday School. Mr Goodwin remembered that Edwards's father had kept an oil-shop in Kingsland Road. He also felt sure that their name in those far-off days had not been Edwards, but precisely what it had been he could not recall.

On this particular occasion Goodwin was out when Edwards called, but his wife was in and they had a long conversation. Edwards asked Mrs Goodwin if her husband was still 'street-walking' and told her, 'I've come to see if I can do you a bit of good. Perhaps it will be an opening for you.' He explained to her that he had just purchased a shop and required someone to manage it for him. Obviously, it needed to be someone whom he could trust; he thought that the Goodwins would be ideal. He then left but promised to call back later and discuss it with her husband.

Edwards clearly had an extremely busy day on 28 November because that evening he returned, as promised, to the Goodwin household and saw Mr Goodwin. In addition to having a long discussion about the shop, Edwards asked his host if he could obtain for him a sash-weight to be used for opening and closing a shop door. It was, he said, for a shop that he owned in York Road, Battersea, a shop that, in fact, existed only in his own fertile imagination.

Two days later, on the 30th, Edwards went once more to Walworth where he had further discussions with the Goodwins about the proposal for their management of the Wyndham Road shop which they were eager to take on. He spent a greater part of the day with them and then stayed the night. The next morning Edwards had breakfast with them. They were somewhat surprised, in view of his claims to the ownership of numerous shops, to discover that he apparently had no money. After breakfast he handed his umbrella to Mrs Goodwin and asked her to pawn it for him; this she did, obtaining the princely sum of 1s-6d for it.

Before finally departing, Edwards collected the sash-weight that Mr Goodwin had obtained at his request. He examined it closely, tested it in his hand for weight and declared that it would do very nicely. He then left, taking the sash-weight with him. That was the morning of 1 December, the last morning that any member of the Darby family were to be seen alive.

Later that morning, Mr and Mrs Goodwin left their home and made their way along the Camberwell Road to its junction with Wyndham Road. It was here that they had arranged to meet Edwards at 11.30. Anxious not to be late, they set out earlier than necessary. This was a mistake; it was cold standing around on the windy street corner and Edwards gave them a long wait, not turning up until five past twelve.

The three of them then walked the short distance to the shop. It was shut but Edwards quickly produced the key and ushered them inside. They had only been in there a few minutes, barely long enough to see the layout, before Edwards suggested that they should go home for some dinner and return at 1.30. All three of them then left the building, Edwards once more locking the door behind him.

Very soon after that, certainly between twelve and one, a pawn-broker called Solomon accepted from a customer a gold watch and chain for which he loaned £7. Mr Solomon was unable to identify Edwards but the duplicate copy of the pawn-broker's contract note (that the customer took away with him) was found in Edwards's possession. The customer had signed his name as W.T. Lowden. The handwriting was that of Edwards and the shop in Wyndham Road traded under the name of W.T. Lowden. The gold watch and chain were the property of William Darby and were being worn by him when he was last seen alive.

At 1.30 p.m. the Goodwins returned to Wyndham Road and found the shop now open for business. Edwards had suddenly obtained money from somewhere because he gave Mr Goodwin 30s to get some clothes out of pawn and 2s to recover his umbrella.

The arrangement agreed for the management of the shop was that the Goodwins should continue to live at their Walworth home but open the shop from eight in the morning until ten at night for which they would be paid 30s a week. It was made clear to them that the rooms on the upper floor of the building were Edwards's private sleeping quarters and at no time, while they were there, did either of them ever penetrate above stairs. At the end of the first week's trading, business having been very poor, their wages were reduced to 20s.

1 December was clearly another extremely busy day for Edwards because, at eight o'clock that evening, he encountered a new and unexpected complication; he received a visit from the landlord of the Wyndham Road premises, John Knight.

Mr Knight, an ironmonger, complained that, on 29 November, Mr Darby had been to see him to discuss a proposal to transfer the tenancy in the event of his selling the business. He had promised to meet Mr Knight again at six o'clock that evening (1 December), but had failed to keep the appointment. Edwards remarked that he knew all about the arrangement but was at a complete loss to understand why Darby had not turned up.

He informed the landlord that he had now completed the purchase of the grocery business and suggested that they might settle the arrangements between them. He was anxious to have the matter agreed quickly as he wished to buy some stock for the shop. Mr Knight had taken an instant dislike to this ferret-faced newcomer, however, and determined that he would not have him as a tenant at any price.

Edwards was told that he would do well not to purchase any stock because he would not be allowed the tenancy. Mr Knight insisted upon seeing Mr Darby and Edwards assured him that he would do so. He said that he felt sure that they could soon sort things out between them and arranged a new appointment for Mr Darby.

Once more Mr Darby failed to keep the appointment. Over the following few days the landlord made repeated visits to the shop in attempts to see his tenant, totally without success. Edwards tried again and again to obtain the tenancy for himself, but Mr Knight would have none of it. The deadlock was finally broken when, on 10 December, Mr Knight finally lost patience, issued a warrant for unpaid rent and then promptly sent in the bailiffs.

By now Edwards had clearly given up all hope of obtaining the tenancy for 22 Wyndham Road and was already turning his attention elsewhere. On 3 December he called on a house-agent, a Mr Hatcher, giving his name as William Darby and enquiring if there were any businesses for sale. He then approached a second agent, in Leyton, with a proposal to acquire the tenancy of 89 Church Road at a rent of 10s a week. He told the landlord of the house, a Mr Basset, that his name was Edgar Edwards and that he owned a grocery business in Barnsbury Road, Islington. Forged references were then provided, one of them in the name of William Darby of Camberwell.

At eleven o'clock on the night of Friday, 5 December, Edwards drove to the Church Road premises in what appeared to be some sort of butcher's cart. He applied to Mr Childs, a milkman who lived nearby, who was less than pleased at being got out of bed, for the keys to the house. The next day he came again and asked Mr Childs whether he knew anyone who could dig the garden over for him. It was suggested to him that Joseph Rawlings at number 79 might be interested in doing it, he being a retired grave-digger, an occupation all too appropriate in the circumstances. When Edwards saw Rawlings and reached an agreement with him to do the job, he instructed him to 'dig it right through and clean all the rubbish away'.

On Monday, 8 December, Edwards made two visits to the house. He first arrived driving a pony and cart containing half-a-dozen condensed-milk boxes which appeared to be filled with books. There was also a large box having a dark cloth top. Later, while Joseph Rawlings was digging the garden, he came again, this time with a four-wheeled van. It had a tarpaulin cover and was loaded with an assortment of furniture and a number of boxes, some of which seemed to be full of yet more books.

Rawlings was asked to carry the boxes into the house which he did with some difficulty because they were rather heavy. There were three of them, two wooden ones and one tin one. Instructed by Edwards, he carried them, one by one, up the stairs and into a bedroom. As he was about to set down the tin one, which was the heaviest of the lot, Edwards told him, 'Put that down steady – there's some valuable crockery in it.' The furniture comprised one bedstead, one or two chairs, a table and a few other odds and ends. While the unloading was going on, Edwards did not say very much, except that his wife would be joining him at the end of the week. His neighbours never did see any woman at the house.

About a week after Edwards had moved into the building one of his neighbours, Mrs Sophia Frear, observed him digging a hole in the garden. The hole seemed to Mrs Frear to be quite extraordinarily deep because, when he stood in it, only his head was visible above ground. When, the following morning, she looked across the gardens again, the hole had been completely filled in and the soil levelled.

Even before he had finished the disposal of the mutilated remains of the unfortunate Darby family, Edwards was already planning his next crime. William Jones, a painter of Commercial Street, was in Whitechapel Road on 9 December when he was approached by a man whom he had first known, over fifteen years before, as Edward Owen.

After the usual civilities, the man asked if Jones could obtain for him a sash-weight of about 5lb. He explained that he needed one for a shop that he owned in Leyton that had a faulty window. He gave Jones 1s, the painter purchased the requested sash-weight and then went with the man, now calling himself Edwards, to a shop in

Church Road, Leyton. He was soon given the job of cleaning the windows, all of which worked perfectly and seemed to be in no need of new sash-weights.

By 19 December the murderous attack on John Garland was quite clearly being planned. Further victims were also in the process of selection. On that day, Edwards approached Charles W. West, an estate-agent in Theobalds Road. He once more called himself W.J. Darby and said that he wished to purchase grocery and provision merchants.

Soon he was paying visits to Ernest Holt, a grocer of Dalston Lane, and Frank Dale, another grocer, this time with a shop in Havant Road. In each case he gave the name of William Darby.

The trial at the Old Bailey, before Mr Justice Wright, was somewhat of a formality. When first told by the police that the bodies of the Darby family had been found and that he was to be charged with their murder, his response had been, 'My good man, I know nothing at all about it.' His attitude in subsequent court hearings had been one of total arrogance. During the hearing at Stratford Magistrates Court, on 27 December, his only concern was the whereabouts of his gold-rimmed pince-nez:

> You gave me permission to retain them on the last occasion – no, no, December 24th – But since then in defiance of that order, the police have deprived me of them in a brutal manner. This officer, Inspector Young, is one of the biggest brutes I have ever seen. I am suffering from his ill-treatment now.

This mixture of arrogance and contempt on the part of the prisoner was one of the principal ingredients of the trial and began when he was asked to plead.

'Do you plead Guilty or Not Guilty?'

Silence.

'Are you Guilty or Not Guilty?'

'You have no business to ask me such a question.'

'You must answer Yes or No.'

'Stuff and nonsense.'

Mr Justice Wright directed that a plea of Not Guilty be recorded.

The prosecution case lasted almost three days and was quite overwhelming. The horrific nature of Edwards's crimes led everyone, however remotely involved, to be not only willing but eager to testify against him and thereby bring him to justice. As a result the prosecution was able, slowly and deliberately, brick by brick, to build up a case against which defence counsel could make only token resistance.

When, at last, counsel for the defence, Mr Hughes, rose to address the packed court he took the only course remaining open to him. He claimed that his client was of unsound mind. He had, he said, only one witness to present but requested that that witness be able to give his evidence with only the judge knowing his true identity.

The reason is that the witness, who is an uncle of the prisoner by marriage and is in a good position in life, has three daughters. One of them is resident in an asylum and the two others are in such a precarious condition mentally that he believes that if it came to their knowledge that they are related to the prisoner it might lead to their losing the balance of their minds.

Mr Justice Wright ruled that he could not comply with counsel's request by ordering secrecy but he had no doubt that the gentlemen of the press would withhold the witness's name from their publications, which indeed they did. After this unusual preamble, apart from revealing that the prisoner's name was really Edward Owen and that some of his relatives were of unsound mind, the mysterious witness contributed almost nothing to the proceedings.

Mr Hughes, in his summing-up on behalf of the defence, claimed that

... the prisoner was insane at the time he committed the act and was, therefore, not responsible for his actions. It is my contention that the crime was committed under an uncontrollable impulse. A person suffering from that form of insanity might not manifest an indication of it to the outside world. The medical men have stated that an uncontrollable impulse might be preceded and succeeded by sane conduct. The enormity of the crime placed it beyond the possibility of being one which could be committed by a sane man. The conception and execution of the plan indicated that it could only have been done by a man incapable of controlling himself.

Mr Justice Wright, in his own summing-up, was less than impressed by this eloquent argument:

The law was that, for the purpose of criminal trials, it must be shown on behalf of a prisoner that he suffered from disease or disorder of the mind which disabled him at the time he committed the crime from understanding the nature and character of the act he was doing. If he understood the nature and character of the act the law said that he was guilty. It was for the Crown to pardon or to commute a sentence if there was any reason for so doing. Was there any ground on which the jury could rightly and truly say that the prisoner was insane? It would be quite easy for the prisoner to have called all or any of the expert witnesses in lunacy whose services were at the command of the Crown; it was not a question of payment. There would not have been the slightest difficulty in producing the evidence.

Still there had been no attempt to call a single witness who would pledge his oath that there was any sign of insanity. Mere unsoundness of mind was not enough. If that were to be recognized as a ground on which juries could act I do not know what would happen to society. If it were to be held that because a crime was ferocious, therefore the person who committed it must be insane, it would be holding out a direct incentive to people who committed crimes to make them ferocious in order that they might be excused on the grounds of insanity.

When Mr Justice Wright completed his summing-up and the jury retired to consider its verdict, it did not detain them very long. Within only a few minutes they returned, filed into their places in the jury-box and sat watching the prisoner as their foreman announced a verdict which surprised no one:

'We find the prisoner Guilty.'

When Edwards was asked by the judge whether he had anything to say as to why sentence of death should not be passed upon him, he replied:

'No. Get on with it, as quick as you like.'

As Mr Justice Wright slowly donned the black cap in preparation for declaring the death sentence, a comment came from the dock:

'It's just like being on the stage.'

Prisoner at the bar. The jury have found the only verdict which was possible according to their oath and their consciences. After a long career of crime in which you have received sentences amounting in all to something like fifteen years' penal servitude and imprisonment, you have been found guilty of committing one of the most terrible murders that can be imagined.

The judge then continued with the traditional words and phrases denoting a sentence of death. The authorities could see no possible reason to disagree and Edwards was accordingly hanged on 28 February 1903.

Whatever views one may have of the ethics of capital punishment, one thing can safely be said about the execution of Edwards. The world was well rid of him.

In a cruel and cold-blooded way he destroyed a young family – and for what? The list of his spoils from the murder of the Darbys comprised a few pieces of furniture, a watch and chain, a wedding dress and a winter coat. He felt no remorse for what he had done, far from it. There can be no doubt whatever that Mr and Mrs Garland were scheduled for the same ruthless destruction. Only the strength and determination of John Garland saved them. Further victims were being lined up. Clearly Edwards believed that he had found a winning formula.

But it is not just the murders themselves that repel. What about his actions afterwards? The real horror is that of carefully cutting and dismembering the bodies and then stowing the pieces away in sacks and boxes. This is the stuff of nightmares. But not, it seemed, to Edwards.

It is not at all surprising that defence counsel argued that no sane man could behave in such an inhuman way. But learned counsel was, in one respect, lucky. At the time and place at which he was speaking – England at the beginning of the twentieth century – it was still possible to believe that sane men do not behave like monsters. The horrors of the Thirty Years' War and the French Revolution were long ago in uncivilized times in the distant past. It was the twentieth century now. At our end of this century it is very different. We have seen far too many monsters and are, alas, no longer so easily shocked or surprised by cruelty and inhumanity.